WAGING PEACE II

WAGING PEACE II

Vision and Hope for the 21st Century

Edited by David Krieger and Frank K. Kelly

The Noble Press, Inc.

Chicago

Printed in the United States of America

Library of Congress Cataloging-in-Publication Data:

Waging peace II : vision and hope for the twenty-first century /
     edited by David Krieger and Frank K. Kelly
          p.   cm.
     ISBN 1-879360-19-5
     1. Nuclear disarmament. 2 Security, International. 3. Peace.
I. Krieger, David. II. Kelly, Frank K., 1914–
JX1974.7.W25   1992   92-50434
327.1'74—dc20   CIP

Noble Press books are available in bulk and discount prices. Single copies are available prepaid direct from the publisher:

The Noble Press
213 W. Institute Place, Suite 508
Chicago, Illinois 60610
800/486-7737

To Ethel R. Wells, an Ambassador of Peace
of extraordinary focus and commitment

CONTENTS

Introduction   xv
David Krieger and Frank K. Kelly

1   **The XIVth Dalai Lama***   1
Our Ultimate Goal

2   **Jacques-Yves Cousteau**   7
Attacking Power with Wisdom

3   **Sir Yehudi Menuhin**   17
The Limits of All "Isms"

4   **Adam Curle**   23
A Spirit of Optimism

5   **Linus Pauling***   29
Reflections on the Persian Gulf "War"

6   **Archbishop Desmond Tutu***   35
God's Dream

7   **Mairead Corrigan Maguire***   47
A Nonviolent Political Agenda for a
More Humane World

8   **Larry Agran**   59
A Peace Conversion Program

9   **Chandler Davis**   71
Science for Good or Ill

10 **Leon Vickman**   89
        Why Nuclear Weapons Are Illegal

11 **Francis A. Boyle**   103
        The Criminality of Nuclear Weapons

12 **Manoutchehr M. Eskandari-Qajar**   121
        The United Nations: Where Should We Go
        from Here?

13 **Jan Tinbergen***   129
        A More Effective United Nations

14 **David Krieger and Robert Woetzel**   147
        A Magna Carta for the Nuclear Age

15 **David Krieger**   177
        Earth Citizenship

16 **Frank K. Kelly**   195
        What Humanity Can Do: The Power of Citizens

Notes

* Nobel Laureate

We will not build a peaceful world by following a negative path. It is not enough to say we must not wage war. It is necessary to love peace and sacrifice for it. We must concentrate not merely on the negative expulsion of war but on the positive affirmation of peace. We must see that peace represents a sweeter music, a cosmic melody, that is far superior to the discords of war. Somehow, we must transform the dynamics of the world power struggle from the negative nuclear arms race, which no one can win, to a positive contest to harness humanity's creative genius for the purpose of making peace and prosperity a reality for all the nations of the world.

In short, we must shift the arms race into a peace race. If we have a will—and determination—to mount such a peace offensive, we will unlock hitherto tightly sealed doors of hope and transform our imminent cosmic elegy into a psalm of creative fulfillment.

MARTIN LUTHER KING, JR.

Even in our sleep
Pain that we cannot forget
Falls drop by drop upon the heart
Until in our own despair
Against our will
Comes wisdom
Through the awful grace of God.

AESCHYLUS

We must be the change we wish
to see in the world.

GANDHI

ACKNOWLEDGMENTS

Thomas Merton once said: "It is a glorious destiny to be a member of the human race." Our experience with the Nuclear Age Peace Foundation has made it evident to us that our directors, advisors, consultants, and members are deeply committed to the service of humanity. With gifts of time, ideas, energy, and money, they have made it possible for this Foundation to survive and grow during a period of revolutionary changes in the world.

This book, like the first in our *Waging Peace* series, reflects many aspects of the expanding projects of our Foundation. It is based upon policies developed by our board members, who now include Wallace T. Drew, Dr. Diana Hull, Nancy Abernathy, Eli Luria, Walter Kohn, Peter Haslund, Charles Jamison, and Ethel R. Wells. We are grateful for the advice and generous support of all these directors.

Our Advisory Council includes some of the most notable leaders in many fields. Members of the Council are Elisabeth Mann Borgese, Hon. Rodrigo Carazo, Rt. Rev. Daniel Corrigan, Adam Curle, Frances Farenthold, Johan Galtung, Elisabeth Kubler-Ross, The XIVth Dalai Lama, Rt. Hon. David Lange, Adm. Gene R. LaRocque, Bernard Lown, Mariead Corrigan Maguire, Alan McCoy, Sir Yehudi Menuhin, Linus Pauling, Hon. Claiborne Pell, Carl Sagan, Stanley K. Sheinbaum, Jan Tibergen, Ted Turner, Archbishop Desmond Tutu, George Wald.

Our consultants give us a continuous flow of helpful suggestions, and many of them are involved in our major projects. The Consultants are Larry Agran, Robert C. Aldridge, Dean Babst, Ian Bernard, Eric H. Boehm, Francis A. Boyle, C. Edward Crowther, John Ernest, M.M. Eskandari-Qajar, Dietrich Fischer, Tibor Frank, Fred H. Knelman, Peter R. MacDougall, Rufus E. Miles, Farzeen Nasri, Jan Øberg, Ronald Shlensky, Dan Smith.

Staff members of the Foundation—particularly Laura Lynch and Ruth Floyd—have poured many hours of intensive work into the on-

going program of the Foundation and have performed essential services in the development of this book.

At the end of the book, we list the names of hundreds of persons in
the United States and other countries who have made financial contributions to support the Foundation's efforts. Their gifts have sustained
us through a decade of action for peace.

INTRODUCTION

When Linus Pauling received the Nuclear Age Peace Foundation's first Lifetime Achievement Award, he had this to say
about war:

> To kill and maim people is immoral.
> War kills and maims people.
> War is immoral.

War is also perhaps the worst imaginable way to settle conflicts. Instead of negotiation, mediation, arbitration, or judicial settlement of
disputes, war relies on the old-fashioned strategy of might makes
right—a strategy that Dr. Pauling and the the authors in this book
would argue is worthy neither of our intelligence nor spirit as a species.

We've all heard of win-win strategies to settle conflicts. War is
generally a lose-lose strategy—except, of course, for the arms mer-
chants.

Since the sixteenth century some 142 million people have died in
wars. Of that number, 108 million or 75 percent have died in wars
during the twentieth century. Since World War II there have been approximately 140 wars and 22 million war-related deaths. Of these
wars, all but two have been fought in developing countries. The two
exceptions were in Hungary and at the Sino-Soviet border. Intervention in these wars in the developing world by major military powers
has been frequent and increasingly covert.

At the beginning of the twentieth century approximately one-half of
all war-related deaths were civilians. By the 1980s the percentage of
civilians killed in warfare had risen to 75 percent. In the active wars
in the 1990s the percentage of civilian war-related deaths has ex-
ceeded 90 percent.

Some say that if you want peace, you must prepare for war, but this
is untrue. If you prepare for war that is what you are likely to get.

If you want peace, you must prepare for peace. This means educating for peace, organizing for peace, researching for peace, working for peace, and building and strengthening institutions at the regional and global levels that will be capable of supporting and maintaining peace.

Peace is far more than the absence of war. It is a positive process of people working together to achieve positive goals. Peace is making it possible that no child dies of preventable causes; it is the eradication of dreaded diseases; it is the overcoming of illiteracy; it is the manifestation of compassion in our communities and in our global village.

The human spirit can rise to higher levels than the celebration of war and so-called victory. We are not biologically predestined to engage in warfare. A group of distinguished scientists issued the Seville Statement on Violence in 1986 as a contribution to the International Year of Peace. They stated that it is scientifically *incorrect* to say:

- that we have inherited a tendency to make war from our animal ancestors;
- that war or any other violent behavior is genetically programmed into our human nature;
- that in the course of human evolution there has been a selection for aggressive behavior more than for other kinds of behavior;
- that humans have a "violent brain";
- that war is caused by "instinct" or any other single motivation.

The Seville Statement concludes: ". . . biology does not condemn humanity to war. . . . Just as 'wars begin in the minds of men,' peace must also begin in our minds. The same species who invented war is capable of inventing peace. The responsibility lies with each of us." [1]

To achieve peace we must care enough about doing so to actively work for peace. If we do not work for peace, others with vested interests—be they economic, political, or social—will win the day with their preparations for war.

In 1938 Bertolt Brecht wrote:

General, your tank is a powerful vehicle.
It smashes down forests and crushes men.
But it has one defect:
It needs a driver.

General, your bomber is powerful.
It flies faster than a storm
    and carries more than an elephant.
But it has one defect:
It needs a mechanic.

General, man is very useful.
He can fly and he can kill,
But he has one defect:
He can think.

We are human beings. We are not tools, automatons, or machines. We can think.

But being able to think does not mean that we will think—at least not deeply enough—about the consequences of our actions. In 1955 Albert Einstein and Bertrand Russell warned that we must not only think, but that we must find "a new way of thinking" or "face unparalleled catastrophe."

If we want to create a future that is peaceful and humane, we must find new ways of thinking and acting. Our planet is threatened by many grave problems including weapons of mass destruction, large-scale environmental hazards, violations of human rights, and overpopulation. To solve these problems will require thought, effort, and determination.

We need to work to reverse our priorities in our own countries from war-oriented to peace-oriented economies and societies. We must, as Martin Luther King, Jr., admonished, "shift the arms race into a peace race."

We must work to strengthen and improve the United Nations and make it live up to its Charter that begins:

WE THE PEOPLES OF THE UNITED NATIONS DETERMINED
to save succeeding generations from the scourge of war,
which twice in our lifetime has brought untold sorrow to
mankind, and

to reaffirm faith in fundamental human rights, in the dignity and worth of the human person, in the equal rights of
men and women and of nations large and small, and

to establish conditions under which justice and respect for
the obligations arising from treaties and other sources of
international law can be maintained, and

to promote social progress and better standards of life in
larger freedom. . . .

For the United Nations to fulfill these lofty goals will require instilling
it with the power to be effective. This will require creating a federal
form of government—similar to the United States changing from the
Articles of Confederation to the Constitution—in which the U.N. has
the power to legislate, collect revenues, and enforce international law.
The General Assembly must become the parliament of the world. In
the same vein, the jurisdiction of the World Court must become compulsory for all nations and an International Criminal Court must be established to deter and punish individuals, including heads of state and
ministers of government, who violate international law. A World Treasury will be needed to collect revenues for a strengthened world organization.

The United Nations Secretary-General should be selected as a
leader of vision and compassion, with a commitment to fulfilling the
mission set forth in the U.N. charter. The Secretary-General should
provide an annual report on the "State of Humanity" with specific recommendations for resolving conflicts peacefully and improving U.N.
activities for common security, environmental protection, economic
development, and resource preservation.

Changes needed to enhance peace and planetary security include the following steps, endorsed by the Nuclear Age Peace Foundation and other organizations:

1. **A COMPREHENSIVE NUCLEAR TEST BAN (CNTB).** When the Partial Nuclear Test Ban was signed in 1963, the parties promised to continue negotiations "to achieve the discontinuance of all test explosions of nuclear weapons for all time." In the aftermath of the Cold War, it is time to conclude these negotiations and agree to end all nuclear testing. The Russians have instituted a unilateral moratorium on nuclear testing and have invited the U.S. to join them.

2. **NUCLEAR NONACQUISITION REGIME.** All proliferation of nuclear weapons must be stopped, including the continued production of nuclear weapons by the current nuclear weapons states. The Nuclear Non-Proliferation Treaty (NPT), which entered into force in 1970, must be strengthened to prevent countries like Iraq and Libya from going nuclear. To do this, the nuclear weapons states must keep the promises they made in Article VI of the NPT "to pursue negotiations in good faith on effective measures relating to cessation of the nuclear arms race at an early date and to nuclear disarmament, and on a treaty on general and complete disarmament under strict and effective international control."

3. **ACCIDENTAL NUCLEAR WAR ASSESSMENT CENTERS.** As long as nuclear weapons exist in our world, we must establish international centers to develop and implement proposals for reducing the risks of accidental nuclear war. As we learned at Chernobyl and Three Mile Island, in every foolproof system, a fool always proves greater than the proof.

4. **MAJOR REDUCTIONS IN ARMAMENTS AND TROOPS.** With the end of the Cold War, major reductions in armaments and troops are possible. These can be accomplished unilaterally or by negotiations. No valid reason exists for the United States to maintain troops in Europe and Japan. The

Center for Defense Information has called for phasing out all 395 U.S. military bases on foreign soil. The program advocated by the Center for Defense Information could reduce annual military spending by one-third, from $300 billion to $200 billion.[2]

5.**INTERNATIONAL CONTROL OF ARMS TRANSFERS.** The five permanent members of the U.N. Security Council are responsible for 80 percent of all arms exports to Third World countries. U.S. weapons sold to Iraq were used against U.S. and allied troops in the Persian Gulf War. The U.N. has recently established an Arms Register to which all arms transfers must be recorded. The next step is to place prohibitions on arms transfers under international law.

6.**A GLOBAL PEACE CONVERSION PROGRAM.** The production of armaments is of little value to a society. With the end of the Cold War, armaments industries should be converted to more socially valuable products. Funding should be made available to encourage the conversion process and to retrain the millions of workers whose livelihood depends upon the arms race.

7.**REVITALIZATION OF THE UNITED NATIONS.** The United Nations is the most important global forum in the world today, but it was established almost fifty years ago under very different conditions than currently exist. There is room for many positive changes in the U.N., including streamlining the bureaucracy, eliminating the veto power in the Security Council, creating a World Treasury and a standing World Security Force. We should also explore changing the one nation/one vote method of voting in the General Assembly to make it more representative of world population and economic power.

8.**AN INTERNATIONAL CRIMINAL COURT AND CODIFICATION OF INTERNATIONAL CRIMINAL LAW.** The International Court of Justice (ICJ) in the Hague is authorized to adjudicate disputes between nations and to give advisory opinions to United Nations bodies and agencies. The ICJ has no jurisdiction over individuals. Thus, we must establish an International Criminal Court with jurisdiction over individuals who commit serious violations of international law, including those defined in the Nuremberg Principles: crimes against peace, war crimes, and crimes against humanity. The Nuclear Age Peace Foundation and the Foundation for the Establishment of an International Criminal Court have proposed a Magna Carta for the Nuclear Age which calls for all individuals, including heads of state and heads of government, to be held accountable under international law.

9. **ANNUAL STATE OF HUMANITY REPORT.** One of the functions of the U.N. Secretary-General should be to prepare and deliver to the people of the world an annual State of Humanity report on the progress being made on the critical issues of peace, environment, development, and human rights.

10. **ACTIVE CITIZENSHIP IN THE NUCLEAR AGE.** The changes called for above are not likely to occur without the involvement of an informed and active citizenry. As citizens of a democracy, we hold the highest office in the land. We are ultimately responsible not only for electing leaders, but for assuring that they behave responsibly in office. To fulfill our responsibility as citizens requires that we be informed. In medicine, physicians are required to obtain the informed consent of their patients before administering treatment. Government officials should be held to the same high standards of informed consent regarding issues of public policy that affect the health, well-being, and future of humanity.

How are these changes to occur? We must begin by fixing them firmly in our minds and hearts and then work with others to achieve them. The dream is peace. It is not an impossible dream, but it does require work to achieve, and it must begin with us. As Gandhi told us, "We must be the change we wish to see in the world." To be this change we must act, as Yehudi Menuhin urges, "in defense of the dignity of life."

For the past five decades, our search for national security has been driven by fear—fear of the Soviets, fear of "subversion," fear of change. But now, the rise of the European Community, the fall of the Berlin Wall, the breakup of the Soviet Union, and many other unprecedented events in recent times have demonstrated both the need and the capacity for change.

We have among us many of the most brilliant people who have ever lived. Let us use our intelligence wisely and move forward into a challenging future with confidence, compassion, and conviction that we can create a just and peaceful world order in the twenty-first century.

The end of the Cold War has provided an unprecedented opportunity to create new structures for peace. Each of the authors in this volume provides a personal vision of what we can do to create a peaceful and just world order. Many of the chapters in this book were first published by the Nuclear Age Peace Foundation as *Waging Peace* booklets. They are collected here as the second volume in the *Waging Peace* series. We hope you find them provocative and a stimulus to join the community of people throughout the world working to realize the vision of peace.

If you would like to know more about the work of the NUCLEAR AGE PEACE FOUNDATION, please write to us at *1187 Coast Village Road, Suite 123, Santa Barbara, CA 93108*.

David Krieger
Frank K. Kelly

THE XIVᴛʜ DALAI LAMA
Our Ultimate Goal

On the surface it appears that humankind has achieved many beautiful things during this century. At the same time, however, a highly advanced technology has posed some serious dangers. I think organizations like the Nuclear Age Peace Foundation have sincerely tried to educate people as to their responsibility in using this technological potential. If it is not used carefully, there could be long-term negative consequences.

War has been a part of human history. In ancient times when wars were fought, there were winners and there were losers. If a nuclear holocaust occurs, however, there will be no winners. Both sides will suffer. In this Nuclear Age, it is very irresponsible for decision makers and heads of state to believe that war is inevitable and then to proceed to prepare for war. We need to find more enlightened and civilized arrangements for resolving conflicts.

In addition to the nuclear threat, our world is facing a suffering economy and a growing population. The message from our shrinking world is, "Be careful and be more harmonious." That's what our planet is showing us.

DEMILITARIZATION

Our ultimate goal or dream should be the demilitarization of the entire planet. I think this goal is possible if proper plans are made and people are educated. Perhaps I am being a bit presumptuous. However, I believe that millions of people feel the way I do, but they are silent. So I speak on behalf of those silent millions.

Receiving the Nobel Peace Prize indicates to me that many people internationally value nonviolence. Therefore, I feel obligated to carry on with my work and speak on behalf of those who support nonviolence.

To achieve demilitarization, our first step should be to denuclearize. Our second step should be to eliminate offensive weapons. And our third step should be to assure that all national forms of military establishments cease to exist. To protect and safeguard humanity, we can create an international force, with all member states contributing.

Demilitarization will save much money because war efforts are very expensive. It makes me sad to see our scientists, the cream of humanity, using their remarkable intelligence for military research. The time and energy of these wonderful people would be much better utilized in a peace effort.

PEACE IS MORE THAN THE ABSENCE OF WAR

Everyone wants peace because war brings us suffering, but peace is not the mere absence of war. It is something more than that. The peace for the last forty-five years in Europe, for example, has been a peace that is the mere absence of war, not a genuine peace. It was fear that created an absence of war, so that was not a genuine peace. The peace that exists there now is, I think, a genuine peace, because this peace comes out of a mutual trust and the realization that we are all brothers and sisters and must live together on this planet. Even if one nation doesn't like another nation, our only alternative is to live together. Under such circumstances, it is much better to live together happily.

On a human level, I think no one wants war. Yet, a genuine peace is something more positive and fuller than the mere absence of war. The elimination of war and military establishments is essential. It is my dream that eventually the United Nations or an organization like it will take the initiative in moving toward real peace. Organizations such as the Nuclear Age Peace Foundation have a certain amount of responsibility in that area, a very special responsibility. Already there exists a nation, Costa Rica, that is demilitarized. That small nation, because of demilitarization, has saved a lot of money and will save even more money to utilize for constructive purposes. Costa Rica's neighbors have spent a lot of money for military equipment. This has led to more fighting and killing.

TIBET AS A ZONE OF PEACE

It is my vision that Tibet should ultimately be a Zone of Peace. In 1987, I made a proposal for a Five-Point Peace Plan. Tibet is geographically quite peaceful, quite fresh and clean. People in that region, due to many factors, are also quite peaceful and friendly. Of course, occasionally Tibetans fight quite fiercely, but generally speaking Tibetan behavior is friendly and peaceful. So, my dream is that Tibet should be a Zone of Peace and protect not only the beauty of our country and culture, but also of the world community.

Foreign visitors travel to Tibet and come away with their mental attitude much changed. They learn many things regarding tranquility and calmness of mind. Even today with the situation very tense and fearful in Tibet—with Chinese soldiers with their rifles or submachine guns ready to shoot—there exists some kind of peaceful nature of mental tranquility. If Tibet were a free democracy and a demilitarized country, I am quite sure it could actually become a sanctuary for peace of mind. People from around the world exhausted from working and a busy life could spend a few weeks in Tibet, get fresh air and clean unpolluted water, and learn techniques to promote peace of mind. This is my dream.

Since these goals and objectives are genuinely peaceful, so should the method of accomplishing these goals be nonviolent. If you use violence you may achieve temporary satisfaction, but in the long run that achievement very often creates other negative consequences. Although nonviolence and human understanding may take more time and require more patience and determination, what you achieve is genuine and has no side effects. It is an achievement gained through mutual understanding.

With this in mind, in 1988 I made another proposal in which I did not ask for a complete separation of Tibet from China. I know the proposal disappointed many Tibetans as many human rights violations are taking place. However, the Chinese population in Tibet has been steadily increasing. According to our information there are now seven million Chinese in Tibet. Already the Chinese population is the majority. So my proposal is a concession to the new majority. Unfortunately, the Chinese government has not responded seriously. So my proposal has had no effect on the other side. On the other hand, many Tibetans are very critical of my proposal and disappointed with the concessions made. I must, therefore, admit the failure of this proposal.

As a result, on 10 March 1991, I made a statement that within a short period I would no longer continue my commitment to this proposal unless the Chinese government showed a new initiative or response. That's how the situation stands now.

We are carrying on this struggle not as antagonists toward the Chinese. We respect China and the Chinese civilization. As a Buddhist monk, I always pray that all beings should be happy. If this is to be an honest prayer, then how can I exclude the well-being of the most populated nation on this planet? We have no ill feelings toward our Chinese brothers and sisters. Free Tibet means to achieve spiritual freedom. That's why I have no problem as a Buddhist monk committing fully to this national struggle. If this struggle were purely political, then I would not join.

I believe that to free Tibet and to allow it to blossom spiritually can no doubt help millions of our Chinese brothers and sisters. This is because communism destroyed the existing Chinese civilization. At the same time, they have completely failed to introduce a new meaningful way of life, a meaningful alternative. The younger generation of Chinese, in particular, remain confused. After all, Buddhism is not something alien to the Chinese mind. That's why I feel a free Tibet can serve our Chinese brothers and sisters.

FIVE-POINT PEACE PLAN

1. The transformation of the whole of Tibet into a Zone of Peace.
2. Abandonment of China's population transfer policy, which threatens the very existence of the Tibetans as a people.
3. Respect for the Tibetan people's fundamental human rights and democratic freedoms.
4. Restoration and protection of Tibet's natural environment and the abandonment of China's use of Tibet for the production of nuclear weapons and the dumping of nuclear waste.
5. Commencement of earnest negotiations on the future status of Tibet and of relations between Tibetan and Chinese peoples.

2 | JACQUES-YVES COUSTEAU
Attacking Power
with Wisdom

SHORT- AND LONG-TERM THINKING

Two events show clearly the significance of short-term and long-term thinking. On March 24, 1989, the *Exxon Valdez* sank off the coast of Alaska, spilling eleven million gallons of oil. On April 8, 1989, a Russian nuclear submarine sank in the Norwegian Sea. Newspapers reported that the *Valdez* was the most catastrophic environmental disaster of all time. It *is* a disaster—for Alaska, for the environment, for the people who make a living from the exploitation of the sea. It is a disaster for the birds, for the sea otters, and for the animals that live in this area of the world. But we lived through a disaster four times greater in quantity in Brittany eleven years ago with the *Amoco Cadiz*. The big lesson of both these oil spills is that, although we suffer tremendous losses initially, oil is basically and fundamentally biodegradable. Ten years from now, the *Valdez* will begin to be forgotten. People will fish again. And even if the environment is slower to recover because of the cold waters, it will recover.

In contrast, the Russian submarine sank in very deep water. There is nothing to see, no visual offense to report. The Russians claim that the fire that caused this disaster did not damage the nuclear furnace, which sank intact. In that case, even if the submarine is not going to be dangerous immediately, it is a time bomb for the future. The submarine will eventually decay. Sooner or later the plutonium or the uranium will leak out. Sooner or later it will threaten our grandchildren, our heirs. And by then they may not even know it is there.

All our attention is focused on a short-term accident, the *Valdez*.

But very little is said about a decaying nuclear submarine in our waters and what it represents.

But there is more bad news. On April 28, 1989, a 274,000-ton tanker, the *Kanchanjunga*, ran aground in the Red Sea, one of the most beautiful places in the world to dive. In the first day alone, 1.5 million tons of oil leaked. The increased incidence of accidents such as this one, the *Valdez*, and the *Valpariso* in the Antarctic is because the transportation of hazardous material is not regulated by appropriate international laws. Rather, various nations have their own regulations. All nations, including the United States and France, are extremely reluctant to delegate even a small parcel of their national sovereignty to an international body that could establish and enforce international regulations for the transportation of hazardous material.

We have talked about oil. But let's consider other dangerous materials, such as tetraethyl lead, that are stored on board ships and transported across the oceans. One major safety problem is that the large ships that carry these hazardous materials, ships that can weigh 250,000 tons, are not very maneuverable. When the crew puts the engines full astern, it takes almost four miles for the ship to stop, which means it may be impossible to avoid a collision. If the captain puts the wheel full to starboard, the ship does not begin to turn for thirty seconds. This inertia of very large ships makes them improper for the transport of dangerous material.

In addition, most of these tankers, although with the *Valdez* this was not the case, travel under a flag of convenience, which enables them to have any crew they want, including the incompetent. The *Valdez* sailed under the American flag. The problem with the *Valdez* crew was that the captain was an alcoholic and the third mate did not have proper certification. But apart from this question of flags of convenience and proper qualification of crews, all ships travel with only one officer on watch on the bridge. Passenger planes are required to have two officers at the wheel, a captain and a co-pilot. When hazardous materials are being transported, there should be two officers on watch on the bridge at all times.

Most tankers also have only a single hull. The *Valdez* had separate tanks, which is almost as good as a double hull, and I understand that the *Kanchanjunga* had a double hull, so the entire load was not lost. But both of them had only one engine, one propeller, and that's wrong when dangerous materials are involved. Both of them had only one steering mechanism, which is also a danger because if it's damaged, then the ship is impossible to control.

There are many rules that should be implemented regarding the transportation of hazardous material. But what about nuclear waste? When one of the old ships that carries nuclear waste from Japan to France, for example, runs aground, what will happen to the tons of plutonium littered on the shore for 250,000 years? In order to avoid such accidents, we have to urgently implement new regulations on the transport of nuclear waste.

There is another danger. During the last year of the Reagan administration, contracts were signed to sell nuclear fuel to Japan. How is it to be transported? By air. Air transport regulations currently prohibit this, but amendments are being prepared to modify the regulations in order to allow transportation of nuclear waste and nuclear material by air—a complete disaster in case of an accident. The concern of the Nuclear Age Peace Foundation and the Cousteau Society is that not enough attention is being given to long-term dangers. And, instead, maybe too much attention is given to immediate events, headlines, the scoop. A big accident is always newsworthy, but the real news is the truth about how those incidents endanger the very existence of our young children. This is what we have to fight to know.

A COMMON DENOMINATOR

A common denominator in every single nuclear accident—at a nuclear plant or on a nuclear submarine—is that before the specialists even know what has happened, they rush to the media saying, "There's no danger for the public." They do this before they themselves know what has happened because they are terrified that the public might react violently, either by panic or by revolt. I think such reactions would be very healthy indeed.

It is striking that the pioneers of the nuclear phenomena have been extremely worried about the consequences of their findings. The first scientist to witness the fission of an atom, Leo Szilard, responded with tears, fearing that the release of such power could fall into the hands of tyrants. Einstein and Oppenheimer had concerns about the use of this energy in war, but even so, the Manhattan Project was created.

In France, there was another kind of reaction. Before the war in 1935, Joliot Curie thought that he had invented the nuclear bomb. He submitted to the Patent Office a public patent about how to make a nuclear bomb. The patent was granted, but a question was posed as to who would get the royalties: the user or the victim? These are the questions we need to ask.

In 1958, I hosted an Atomic Energy Agency meeting in Monaco on the subject of the disposal of nuclear waste. There were many atomic technicians who defended nuclear electricity by saying, "The waste will be a problem, but we have to proceed because we will later find a way to deal with this." That's the syndrome of Saint Exupery. Saint Ex believed we would always find a way to correct the damage we have created. But to build a machine before there is a way to control it is, of course, criminal.

During this meeting, a very famous American scientist from the National Academy of Sciences had lunch in my home. My mentor, Louis Fage, was also there. The American scientist defended the future of nuclear energy, saying to me, "Jacques, this energy is necessary for humankind, and we will build it, even at the cost of closing all the oceans to human activity." We were terrified. Louis Fage came out of this lunch as white as an aspirin tablet.

TAKING ACTION

Soon after that, the French government decided to dump nuclear waste from Marcoule into the Mediterranean. At the Oceanographic Institute in Monaco, and under my direction, none of us slept for several weeks. We were busy alerting the residents of every single village and town on the route of the train that nuclear waste was to be carried to the harbor of Marseille and dumped into the ocean. The campaign was so successful that thousands of people lay down on the train tracks from Marcoule to Marseille. The train was obliged to go back with its villainous cargo. The hangar in which they had to store the nuclear waste is still called the Cousteau Hangar. I did not give them authorization for the name, but that's okay.

As a consequence of this, I met with the Atomic Agency in Vienna and signed an agreement to host the International Marine Radioactivity Laboratory at the Oceanographic Institute in Monaco so that, at least, I could know what was happening. The laboratory studied the effect of the bioconcentration of nuclear products in the food chain and showed how the concentrations could be dangerous for people.

Then came the fury about the breeder reactor. Creys-Malville in France was the site chosen on which to build the Phoenix and then the Superphoenix, the first nuclear breeders for energy exploitation. Of course, I was among the most violent objectors.

We organized demonstrations on the site, but French police used tear gas to disperse us, and the Superphoenix was built. Less than one year after its completion, a tremendous leak occurred in the liquid sodium tank that was supposed to cool the breeder, and the reactor was shut down. For more than one year, the leak could not be corrected. Finally officials decided to reactivate the breeder reactor without the sodium tank by using emergency cooling chains of sodium, a decision that represents a tremendous danger.

These incidents seem to be an internal affair for France, but they represent an international threat, as was the case for the famous accident at Chernobyl. It was also the case in America with Three Mile Island, but Chernobyl was more serious, a real disaster. Even so, the Soviet Central Agency for the Safety of Population Against Radiation reassured communities that they were not in danger even before the experts knew what was going on. And they continued to do so until recently. But in Monaco, we measured the fallout from Chernobyl on the south of France and could guarantee that, at least at that time, there was a danger for the people of the south of France. A number of farm products were too dangerous to consume but were consumed later because of reassuring communiqués.

THE TRAGEDY OF THE TECHNOCRATS

The tragedy is that those technocrats believe that the public is not able to understand problems, that we are children and have to be talked to like ignorant children, that the technocrats are the only ones who know what to do. But the truth is, it is the technocrats who don't know what they are doing.

There is, in France, a new nuclear plant being built in Nogent, fifty-five or sixty miles from Paris on the Seine River. News of this construction, after the accident at Chernobyl, was very disquieting for the population of Paris because an accident in Nogent would be a complete disaster for all of Paris. My friends from a French television channel interviewed the director of the plant in a segment to be shown at the end of a documentary on Chernobyl. They asked the Nogent plant director what the plan was in case of an accident. He said, "Oh, here an accident is not possible, of course." The interviewer responded, "But if it were, Paris would be impossible to evacuate." The director said, "Oh, yes, I know. We can't evacuate Paris." "Then what will you do?" The director scratched his head and said, "Well, we will give advice to the public." "What kind of advice?" "Well, for example, to close their windows."

How have we arrived at this low point in the long process of developing nuclear energy? Was there really that fast a need for nuclear energy? Is the uranium fission system of generating energy the only one? No. There are others, and they have not been developed. They have not even been studied in depth. Why? Because the first application of nuclear science was the bomb that exploded on Japan, and that heritage is spoiling everything else. The military developed nuclear energy by uranium fission because it yields uranium and plutonium, which are the fuel for bombs. By developing civilian nuclear energy, they are camouflaging part of the expense of the nuclear bomb, an expense that would be too great a strain on the military budget for any Parliament or Congress to vote for it.

Then came the testing of bombs because they wanted to make hydrogen bombs and multimegaton bombs. In 1962 and 1963, the Russians started atmospheric tests, and a year later the Americans began the same series of nuclear tests. In Monaco we had a laboratory to measure radioactivity in the air and in rainwater. The first time nuclear tests in the atmosphere were conducted, we tested for it and noted the measured radioactivity on a piece of paper taped to the wall. But very quickly, our measurements went off the paper and all the way up the wall to the ceiling. We knew that the levels of radioactivity in the atmosphere and in rainwater were extremely dangerous for humankind in 1962 and 1963.

THE LIVES OF 50,000 CHILDREN

In 1965 I invited Professor Zenkevitch, the president of the National Academy of Sciences of the Soviet Union and a member of the Advisory Committee of the Oceanographic Institute to have lunch with me at UNESCO. He was a fine gentleman, fluent in several languages. Four of us had lunch, and we spoke about many things, mainly oceanography. After cheese, we had ice cream. I couldn't wait any more and asked Zenkevitch, "Why did you do those [nuclear] tests? Did the Academy of Sciences make the government aware of the consequences of those tests?" He looked at his ice cream and answered, "Yes, the government asked the opinion of the Academy of Sciences. We worked on the project and warned the government that it would probably cost the lives of 50,000 children in the USSR alone. The government answered us that if they did not make the tests, it would possibly cost many more lives." And then he wept, and I still see his tears falling into his ice cream.

THE PROBLEM TODAY

The problem today is to know if science is going to be able to develop a way of getting energy from nuclear reactions without making bombs and waste, to use nuclear science for the benefit of people without the danger of nuclear waste, without the danger of bombs.

The problem is to get rid of the arrogance of technocrats. We want to know the truth when an accident occurs. And we want to fight. We want to give the right to all people to decide what risks they will or will not take, to protect the quality of life for future generations.

A BILL OF RIGHTS FOR FUTURE GENERATIONS
(The Cousteau Society is actively pursuing the adoption of this Bill of Rights for Future Generations.)

The General Assembly,

Mindful of the determination proclaimed by the peoples of the world in the Charter of the United Nations to reaffirm faith in the dignity of the human person and to promote social progress and better standards of life in larger freedom,

Acknowledging that it is among the purposes of the United Nations to achieve international cooperation in solving international problems and to be a center for harmonizing the action of nations in the attainment of these common ends,

Recognizing that for the first time in history the rights of future generations to exercise options with respect to the nurture and continuity of life and the enrichment and diversity of their mental and physical environment are seriously threatened,

Believing that the preservation and promotion of these rights has a claim on the conscience of all peoples and all nations,

Convinced that each generation has the inherent right to determine its own destiny and the corresponding responsibility to accord a similar right to future generations as an extension of the right of the living,

Solemnly Proclaims the necessity of securing the universal recognition of this right and their responsibility; and to this end,

DECLARES THAT:

ARTICLE 1.
Future generations have a right to an uncontaminated and undamaged Earth and to its enjoyment as the ground of human history, of culture, and of the social bonds that make each generation and individual a member of one human family.

ARTICLE 2.

Each generation, sharing in the estate and heritage of the Earth, has a duty as trustee for future generations to prevent irreversible and irreparable harm to life on Earth and to human freedom and dignity.

ARTICLE 3.

It is, therefore, the paramount responsibility of each generation to maintain a constantly vigilant and prudential assessment of technological disturbances and modifications adversely affecting life on Earth, the balance of nature, and the evolution of mankind in order to protect the rights of future generations.

ARTICLE 4.

All appropriate measures, including education, research, and legislation, shall be taken to guarantee these rights and to ensure that they not be sacrificed for present expediencies and conveniences.

ARTICLE 5.

Governments, non-governmental organizations, and individuals are urged, therefore, imaginatively to implement these principles, as if in the very presence of those future generations whose rights we seek to establish and perpetuate.

3 | SIR YEHUDI MENUHIN
The Limits of All "Isms"

The situation in former Yugoslavia presents an overwhelming opportunity for us to usher in and to inaugurate the next phase in the evolution and structuring of ethnic, social, and political entities in the context of intercultural, interpeoples relationships.

The territorial ethnic wars now seizing the former composite state represent the lingering conceptual prisons of nineteenth-century thought, such as the concept of "sovereign national states," which has resulted in the suppression of minorities or subservient peoples; the defense of arbitrarily established borders, borders rarely corresponding to natural demarcations, ethnic, linguistic, or geographical; the whole panoply of power, weapons, automated men, and, more recently, women and children; and independent "foreign" policies, which mirror shifting and uneasy alliances and treaties and result in ever more destructive wars.

Mentalities have not yet evolved from the single-track concept of the all-inclusive, all-exclusive enclosing wall, the sacrosanct deity demanding the constant sacrifice and death of its trapped inhabitants, and the multitract concepts corresponding to the disposition of real people, more or less different or similar, with their many levels of interaction, corresponding to cultural, geographical, climatic, commercial, and historical patterns.

At the very least, the cultural, which represents the *inner* life of a community, its language, art, history, living patterns, schools, churches, styles, music, etc., must be kept distinct from a community's *outer* connections. It is very much the same with any individual. The most hateful aspect of any tyranny is its determination to eliminate, to control our inner life.

I would suggest that the European Community forthwith recognize the many cultures of former Yugoslavia as distinct entities, each with a *central* district, and that the European Community adopt each as a ward, to be respected and cared for but *not* to be recognized as sovereign nations, a misnomer.

The members of the distinguishable ethnic entities should each be entitled to respect and recognition, whether grouped together in one region, dwelling as minority pockets in other regions, or living as dispersed or nomadic exiles with no region of their own (for instance Kurds or Gypsies).

Border regions or areas with mixed populations should be patrolled by police units composed of at least the two ethnic groups involved. The teams should consist of two or more people willing and trained to work together to guard their common peace and to promote mutual respect.

Border regions should have common telephone numbers, at least for emergency, fire, and postal services.

A EUROPEAN DEFENSE SERVICE

Recognition of the ethnic entities by the European Community and of their rightful individual cultural autonomies would carry the obligation to provide a European defense service composed of small groups of men—say ten or twelve—from many different European ethnic cultures, *excluding* the particular one they may be assigned to patrol. The groups should be well trained together over a sufficiently long period—perhaps a few years—and the members could be recruited from special military academies or from institutions of higher learning. Their task would be to disarm or demobilize the local forces, including tanks, artillery, and all weapons, excepting those required for local policing, described above, or belonging to a European military presence.

It is, of course, essential that all armed services, i.e., these small teams of both categories, be constituted of persons of a certain moral quality, as the respect in which they will be held and the gratitude shown them will depend far more on the example they set in behavior and guidance than on their military prowess.

This essential recognition of a human being's inalienable right to his own or to a culture of his choice, or to several cultures of his choice, would constitute the first elements of a Parliament of Cultures. This organization could serve as a model to be adopted by or extended to the larger and smaller new cultures, the "Republics" of the new Russian Commonwealth, the Eastern European nations, or other parts of the world hideously menaced with genocide, tyranny, and civil war.

This European initiative of putting the Europeans and their Community and Parliament at the service of our fellow Europeans should enjoy the support and cooperation of the United Nations and NATO. These organizations might apply these ideas to other areas.

Having briefly discussed the handling of our "inner" cultural problems, I would like to discuss the spatially larger "outer" dimensions. These concern relations between peoples, particularly where cultures meet and converge, as they do along borders. Once peace is established in these areas through the presence of the mixed, trained, and exemplary policing units I have suggested, perhaps a degree of cooperation for services requiring the joint participation of adjacent neighborhoods will be more readily agreed upon.

Thus, joint services in the departments of health, post, fire, etc., could be instituted on a wider level in Europe and on a global scale.

This initiation to intercultural activity would prepare for a more enlightened participation in the handling of many world problems, such as environmental pollution, education, and social and psychological difficulties.

Offering guidance along these lines should be an obligation of those community men and women particularly experienced and qualified in matters such as pollution, industrialization (where today enormous discretion is required), banking (dominated today by downright stupidity and cupidity), unemployment versus leisure time (two manmade and artificial problems), general safety, reverence for life (largely lacking), transport and world trade, and the *cautious* use of credit.

At *all* levels—crafts, arts, education—the forming of the whole human being must be discussed and teaching and training in all aspects of human achievement encouraged—from music to sport, in broad amateur as well as narrower professional approaches.

A COMMON RESPECT FOR LIFE

The European Community itself should not be a club of the equally affluent, excluding rural economies or even different approaches to administration. Its members can be constitutional monarchies or not, or differ in other ways, presidential system versus parliamentary, for we *need* variety and a certain amount of experimentation, but above all the members must demonstrate a common respect for life, including human life.

Each culture must be distinctive and as such bring a specific contribution to the whole; this is the truly European character. Determination, rigidity, and uniformity are called for in such matters as the banning of pesticides and battery farming; the development of high-speed, nonfriction railways running in semivacuum tunnels between all European capitals; space exploration; the preservation of species, rain forests, and the oceans; and also for the establishment of a common well-reasoned, enlightened foreign policy. These are all subjects and areas for our *outer* lives, since they impinge on the outer lives of all life on Earth, including the lives of our children, *their* children, and of our collective future.

SOVEREIGNTY IS OUTDATED

The nineteenth-century concept of "sovereign nations" is totally outdated; it is in no way capable of fulfilling either our *inner* or our *outer* needs. It has become a dangerous, often evil relic of the transition from traditionally based small states to the larger powers that were required to deal with growing industrial capacity, growing volume of trade, growing millions of peoples no longer bound by agricultural toil or tradition, and growing firepower, and the need to control and direct ever larger masses of people, either by education, indoctrination, opportunity, promise, punishment, encouragement, sheer brutal oppression, or by war.

The "sovereign" state, while remaining the vessel of great historical development, must give way to two self-balancing developments: the ethnic regional or dispersed or nomadic entity on the one hand and the federal or collective (or commonwealth) on the other, the one smaller than the "state," the other larger, and each having its own structures and administrations, its own *raison d'être,* and its own parliament, executive, and judiciary, with coordination between the three present—call them, for convenience's sake, Local, States, and Federal.

I have tried to outline the immediate steps and measures as well as the ultimate purpose and direction to cope with present situations.

I have traced the great lines without going into myriad details, for what I feel so deeply today is a need for a realistic and positive vision for the future, something that is altogether lacking in our era, propelled as it is from one emergency to the next without foresight or preparation and without a vision of where we may be advancing to.

We are now learning the limits of *all* "isms," of all theories, but it is no reason for us to become cynics. Rather, we must redefine what is important to live for, to sacrifice for, to be grateful for, and to fight for.

4 | ADAM CURLE
A Spirit
of Optimism

I am now seventy-six and for the last four and a half decades I have been involved to some extent in the affairs of the world beyond the narrow boundaries of my own country, England. During this period much of my time has been spent on the problems of poverty, and in the last quarter century, of conflict, mainly but not exclusively in what we have come to call the Third World. Some of this time I lived with my family in Asia and Africa, and even when I did not, I was constantly traveling to one troubled area or another.

During most of this time, though naturally optimistic and, I hope, positive by temperament, I was intellectually pessimistic. I did not see how the monstrous global diseases of poverty and violence could be cured. It seemed to me that the forces trying to overcome these ills were so much weaker than those promoting them.

FEAR AND GREED

These malign forces, as I saw them, were institutionalizations of very widespread human tendencies: fear and greed. These, in turn, derived from equally widespread illusions about our own nature, that it was bad and that we were separated from each other. (And I suppose my own basic optimism came from the belief that human nature was fundamentally good and that we were all joined by our common humanity; but of course these differences are not clear-cut.)

The tendencies of fear and greed have, I imagine, always existed, but they began to crystallize as institutions around the end of the Middle Ages. It was then that the nation-state as we know it, with a centralized government and a bureaucracy, began to emerge. This process included the emergence of national armed forces (previously kings wanting to wage war had needed to borrow the retainers of their nobles, who might then want them back at harvest time—or to use them to rebel against the king!), which perhaps provided an environment that favored business enterprise, because it was at this time that the great banking houses developed, the Fuggers, the Banco Giro of Venice, and so on. Governments profited from these new financial arrangements, and one of the roles of the new armies was to protect and expand them. Science and technology came to be practiced less as hobbies for gentlemen than as tools of industry and the military.

Finally, a new philosophy came into being. The teachings of John Calvin were taken by some to suggest that worldly success was somehow an indication of divine favor. The Church previously had been, at least officially, against the taking of interest. Now, however, since it was regarded as a means of increasing wealth, taking interest was deemed to be good. This philosophy has had an immense impact. Why? I think because those persons riddled with self-doubt and self-loathing now had an objective means of proving—to themselves and to others—that they were good.

These material and spiritual concepts, which began around five hundred years ago, have now crystallized. The vast military-industrial complexes, the enormous military machines, the crazed belief in "defense" that shatters the economies of rich and poor alike, the enormous transnational corporations spreading like ineradicable parasites through both friend and foe, the mania for growth, the worship of acquisition and the market, and nation-state arrogance and the transcendent belief in the importance of national interests—these, I thought, had become the forces that ruled us.

Or most of us. As individuals we might not be utterly subjected, but how could we live without to some degree truckling to theses forces—our local bank, the supermarket, the taxes we pay for the government to buy guns?

And most countries were dominated by these forces. The Scandinavians, Costa Ricans, and perhaps a few others were honorable exceptions.

THE MATERIALISM VIRUS

But the materialism virus has spread. Even where the technology has not yet reached, the ideology has. When I visited remote villages as an apprentice anthropologist fifty years ago I found that those people most respected were not the rich—they might have been envied, but they were often hated, for good reason, or feared. Rather, the people looked up to the devout, the hospitable, the tellers of good stories, the wise old men. Now it is the man who has made good in business and as a result owns a refrigerator, a car, or even a pair of shoes who is respected.

So, although I began by speaking of developments in the "West," I have to say that these developments are global, at least at the national level—there are, of course, communities that have escaped the infection. The state machinery is everywhere much the same, however different the culture of the people may be.

Of course there is another side to this gloomy picture. Especially since World War II, a wonderful international structure has arisen. The United Nations, with its host of specialized agencies large and small and a vast number of nongovernmental agencies, of which the Nuclear Age Peace Foundation is an admirable example, has tried to meet the world's dire need with impartial charity. But it has not been enough. The rich nations, except when their own interests were served, have stood shamefully aloof. The United States and my country, Britain, have hated and withdrawn support from the United Nations because they did not necessarily support the U.N.'s purposes and policies (and for the same reason Britain has been very dubious about "joining" Europe). Even the aid these countries have given covertly served their own objectives rather than those of the recipients. They fawned on loathsome tyrannies for venal or "ideological" reasons.

I saw much of this. No wonder I was intellectually gloomy, even if inwardly still buoyant.

THE QUEST FOR PEACE

Things then began, mysteriously, to change. Approximately twenty years ago I began to feel an expansion of awareness. So did countless others, many of them several years earlier. What it was is easier to describe in poetry than prose; I can only suggest that it was an opening of the boundaries of my self to an infinitely vast Self that contained—increasingly—the selves of all other beings. This transformed my feelings about almost everything—the work I was doing, the people I met, race, development, my students, the violent conflicts I was attempting to mediate. Increasingly I devoted myself to the quest for peace.

Outwardly not much changed in the world for several years. Then came Gorbachev. He simply said what every sensible human being had known for years: that the Cold War, with its deadly build-up of lethal weapons and ludicrous waste of resources, was absurd; why not stop it? But he said it in a manner and at a level that were irresistible. And with the end of the Cold War came changes in Eastern Europe that are both encouraging and pose great new dangers and problems. It all happened with unbelievable speed.

For me, however, there are now also intellectual grounds for optimism. The dreadful concatenation of state, military, economic, and other factors has been shaken loose. It no longer has such a psychological or indeed material stranglehold on our thinking. (One reason why Margaret Thatcher had to go was that her ideas remained stuck in the old pattern.)

But a great deal more must still happen quickly. The priorities are aid to the South, which is crippled by debts, local conflicts, poverty, and famine—things that will not all be automatically remedied by changes in Northern policies; the destruction of all stocks of nuclear weapons and, of course, an end to nuclear proliferation and testing; a conclusion to the disgustingly lucrative arms trade; effective mediation of ethnic conflict in formerly Communist-dominated areas; strengthening of the United Nations mandate accompanied, of course, by some weakening of national sovereignty—for example, the U.N. must be given some mandate for involvement in internal conflict; and a global agreement on measures to check environmental deterioration, such as the destruction of the rain forests and the massive use of fossil fuels.

Without firm action on these fronts (the military term, though partly inappropriate, illustrates the urgency and force required), our hopes for a more just, humane, and peaceful order may be shattered. On some fronts the dangers are already far advanced, such as the spread and use of nuclear weapons, famine, biospheric damage, unpredictable perils spawned by desperation in the Third World, violence in parts of Europe and the former USSR, AIDS, drugs, and alienation and social breakdown in the great cities.

THE GREAT STRUGGLE

The great struggle, however, is less between the need for right action and the practical difficulties of achieving it, than between the spirit of awareness sensed twenty years ago and the vested interests, material and emotional, of the past.

The amazing tempo of recent developments and the absolute necessity for equal rapidity in resolving the persisting obstacles to real peace has daunting portents for the future. My grandchildren may see a wonderful world that we can hardly imagine—just as we couldn't imagine the destruction of the Berlin Wall. Or they may see the collapse of all comfort and security that is equally hard for us to envisage (unless we live in Southern Sudan, the Jaffna Peninsula, Mozambique, Yugoslavia, or an inner-city slum).

But the spirit, I feel, is surging in the hearts of countless people released from various bondages, inner and outer; perhaps those still bound will soon seek to join them. Herein lies my hope, rational I trust, for humanity and for the planet.

5 | LINUS PAULING
Reflections on the
Persian Gulf "War"

On the 8th of January, 1991, I bought a quarter page in the *New York Times* and published an advertisement, "STOP THE RUSH TO WAR!" Instead of going to war, the advertisement argued, let's continue applying pressures—economic pressures and other pressures on Iraq—rather than go ahead and wage a war that would cause a great amount of human suffering. I didn't expect it to be effective, but I felt that it was my duty to do what I could. So I did by publishing that advertisement.

TO KILL AND MAIM PEOPLE IS IMMORAL

On the 18th of January, after the war had started, I published another advertisement. I didn't have money enough to buy another quarter page in the *New York Times*, but for a third of the money I got a quarter page in a Washington, D.C., paper. Another paper published the advertisement and charged me only one dollar. The advertisement was an open letter to President Bush. It started out, "To kill and maim people is immoral. War kills and maims people. War is immoral. Stop the war. Resort instead to continuing to apply pressures of various sorts. Cancel the ultimatums. Begin discussions, not only of Kuwait but of the great world problems in general."

One of my complaints about President Bush was that he said that he refused absolutely to discuss any other questions than just withdrawal from Kuwait, and that one of the ultimatums was that the rich Arab family that formerly owned the country was to be restored to ownership of the country. He had given up saying anything about democracy because he knew that Kuwait wasn't a democratic country, with only a few percent of the people in Kuwait having the right to vote.

Also, our policy had been to refuse to enter into discussions of the Palestinian problem—which, of course, was one of the points that Saddam Hussein was raising. It's a disgrace that the Palestinian problem should remain unresolved so many decades after it arose and it has become exacerbated.

So the war went on. My open letter to President Bush probably didn't make any difference at all. I was thinking, what is going to happen now? I wasn't very smart. Part of the reason was that I had stopped working on military explosives when the second World War came to an end, and I hadn't kept up with the developments that had been occurring in this field. That's the excuse I had for not having foreseen what was going to happen.

The war went on. In the first days we pretty well destroyed the aviation facilities of Iraq. We continued to bombard Iraq and, after some weeks, the war stopped without any extensive ground war having been undertaken. It was almost an entirely aerial war with only 150 Americans killed. I was glad about that. Four hundred thousand Americans were killed in the second World War and, of course, millions of other combatants—some 50 million people died as a direct result of the war.

I was reading about an event that took place forty-seven years ago on the 6th of June, 1944—the landing in Normandy when the American, British, and Canadian forces, with a few Free French forces, landed on the coast of Normandy. Tens of thousands of young soldiers were killed in that landing. One unfortunate regiment suffered 25 percent casualties on the first day. The average age of the American soldiers there was nineteen. The average age of the German soldiers was seventeen. They had been fighting a long time and were having trouble finding anybody to fight on the front. These young people who had not yet had a chance to enjoy and experience life were sent off to die by the old people who decide that there will be a war.

In the Korean war, 54,000 Americans were killed. In the war in Vietnam, 58,000 Americans were killed, and some hundreds of thousands were wounded, and millions of the enemy were killed. We withdrew and negotiations ultimately began after that much loss of life.

THIS WASN'T A WAR

So, I was thinking that we're going to have a ground war and perhaps after 50,000 Americans have died, we'll begin negotiating, talking about the problems. That didn't happen, and the reason that it didn't happen was something that I should have been able to foresee but didn't. There were 150,000 aerial sorties against Iraq, so great damage was done by our Air Force and some by shells shot over from the battleships.

There wasn't much response. Why wasn't there much response? We had sold maybe a billion dollars worth of machines of war—planes and tanks and missiles of various sorts—to the Iraqis during the Iran-Iraq conflict, when we were supporting Iraq and opposing Iran. In the meantime, another trillion dollars were spent by President Reagan on changing our military machine. Great effort and great amounts of money were expended. So they had in Iraq, and we knew that they had, the old military machines, and we had new ones against which the old ones wouldn't be very effective. That's what happened. As I say, I should have been smart enough to realize that that was going to happen.

I am sure that President Bush and the people in the Pentagon and the top consultants and advisors in Washington knew that that was the situation. They knew about how superior our weapons of warfare were, especially aerial warfare, and what was going to be the outcome. What did it result in? One hundred fifty Americans killed. How many Iraqi people—soldiers and civilians, old people, young people, children, babies—died? The one piece of evidence that I have is the 150,000 aerial sorties. During the second World War in these aerial sorties the average weight of bombs carried and dropped was 2.3 tons per sortie, and three million tons of high explosives were dropped and there were three million people killed. One person was killed per ton of high explosive bomb dropped. That probably is about right for the attack against Iraq.

I don't have much information. You remember there was one scud missile that carried a little less than a quarter of a ton of high explosives that killed twenty-seven Americans when it exploded. So that was much higher, a hundred times as high as the average of one death per ton of high explosive. That means that some 300,000 Iraqis were killed. Iraq hasn't been willing to state what the number of their deaths was and, at present, the United States hasn't released any of our estimates of the number killed. In the earlier wars, we were releasing a statement everyday about how many of the enemy were killed.

Three hundred thousand killed. What does that mean? Three hundred thousand. One hundred fifty Americans were killed—two thousand Iraqis were killed per one American killed. That means that this wasn't a war. In a war you have opposing forces that fight and there are deaths on both sides and finally one side wins. In the old days perhaps this was a demonstration of the democratic process—the side with the biggest number of fighters won. This wasn't a war. This you could call a massacre or slaughter, perhaps even murder.

WHAT DOES THE FUTURE HOLD?

I am depressed about the fact that the United States carried out this action. Though it's been done, and perhaps it will be done again, what is the future going to hold? There are two things that might happen. First, it may be that the situation with respect to weapons will be sort of frozen. A second possibility is that the weapons that we've brought over there will not be brought back to the United States, but will be sold to the highest bidders—another source of income. And we'll perhaps spend another trillion dollars to develop the next generation of smart weapons so that we would still be ahead in the way that we were ahead in the fight with Iraq.

Whichever way it happens, we have to recognize that now the United States is the one strong power on Earth and President Bush has talked about the new order that we're going to have. There are two possibilities about the new order. One is that we'll have a continuation of the policy that, if there is some country that behaves in a way that we don't like, we'll go in and kill a good number of the people there, perhaps three hundred thousand if it's a good-sized country with some 20 million inhabitants like Iraq. We'll do it in such a way that we have practically no losses and we'll get the sort of government put in that we like, as we did in Grenada or Panama. Grenada had very little in the way of a military machine, and there weren't very many casualties. In Panama there were some thousands of people killed. So that's one possibility—a rule by terrorism in the world.

I looked up terrorist in the dictionary. I'm a sort of dictionary buff and have been for sixty years. It was in 1931 that reporters started asking me what my hobbies were and I said "Well, I collect dictionaries and encyclopedias." I've been doing that now for sixty years. Terrorists are people who make an ultimatum, a demand of some sort in the form of an ultimatum threatening to kill hostages or other people if the demand is not met. What did President Bush do? He issued some ultimatums that were absolute, that by a certain date the Iraqis would have to withdraw from Kuwait or else. And "or else" consisted in our killing 300,000 Iraqis, two thousand to one. It seems to me that our country has become a terrorist country on a very large scale.

TOWARD A FUTURE WORTHY OF OUR INTELLIGENCE

What is the alternative? The alternative, I think, has been expressed in my statement that war is immoral, to kill and maim people is immoral. The alternative would be for the United States to say, "We are a moral country." We dominate the Earth and are the greatest country on Earth—although not the one in which the health of the people is the greatest, or the infant mortality is the least, or the distribution of wealth is the best. At any rate, we are a moral country.

We are going to apply pressures to the extent that we can on any other country in the world that behaves in an immoral way. These pressures would not be terrorist threats to attack and kill a certain fraction of the population. Rather, they would be pressures of a different sort, some of which, of course, tend to border on the immoral, such as interfering with food coming into the countries so that people begin to starve in the country against which there is an embargo. This is not nearly so immoral as killing large numbers of people.

I hope that the Nuclear Age Peace Foundation will work in the effort to make the United States into a moral country that could lead the world into a future of morality, a future worthy of man's intelligence.

6 ARCHBISHOP DESMOND TUTU
God's Dream

The first few chapters of the Bible in the book of Genesis were not designed to provide us with scientific information. They are much more like poetry than prose, highly imaginative writing because, from the nature of the case, no one was contemporary with the events of the beginning on any showing. Consequently we should expect that those stories were providing us not with scientific truth, such as is readily available in a textbook on paleontology or geology, but much more with existential religious truth, truth about what is ultimate relating to God, ourselves, the universe we inhabit and the rest of God's creation.

Who can doubt that the Bible is right on when it describes the devastating consequences of human sin when we look at the ecological disasters that are due to our wanton consumption of irreplaceable fossil fuels, our irresponsible pollution of our rivers and the atmosphere with our careless use of aerosol sprays containing chlorofluorocarbon gases that are damaging the ozone layer, and all that we are doing to produce the greenhouse effect; and when we look on nature, red in tooth and claw, the Bible having spoken symbolically about Adam crushing the serpent's head whilst it would forever seek to bruise his heel? Who can doubt that things are horribly out of joint when we see the laws of the jungle applied so ruthlessly in the intercourse between humans, where it is eat or be eaten, survival of the fittest, and the weakest to the wall.

We have made high virtue of a callously selfish competitive spirit that would fain wipe the floor with one's rivals in the perennial rat race, where stomach ulcers have become status symbols. We set a high premium on success. We do not much care what a person succeeds in as long as he or she succeeds. The worst thing that can happen to anyone is to fail. Human beings have come to be valued not for what and who they are, persons of infinite value, a value intrinsic to who they are and which is due to nothing they have done or failed to do. It is a value with which they are endowed simply because they are human beings created in the image of God. We are at one another's throats in a ghastly kind of way, most graphically represented by the arms race and especially by the threat of a nuclear holocaust. But was this inevitable and is it inexorably to remain as such, so that we can look forward to nothing more pleasant than to be incinerated in a nuclear explosion that will probably leave nothing worthwhile in its wake?

GOD'S INTENTION

The Bible has another picture. It describes what it believes was God's intention for his creation, and it is found in those exquisite stories I referred to that are found at the beginning of the book of Genesis. There it speaks about how God created all there is, preparing it for man's habitation. And this was the beautiful garden of Eden. Everything was lovely in the garden. Adam lived in perfect harmony with the animals. The lion played happily with the frisky lamb. There was not bloodshed in God's garden, not even for religious sacrifice because everyone in God's garden was vegetarian. Adam enjoyed his work tending God's garden because his work was recreative and wholesome and not a drudgery.

Did I say everything was lovely in the garden? Not quite. God noticed that his friend and human creature was not quite happy. Solicitous as ever God said, "It is not good for man to be alone." God suggested that Adam should choose a friend and mate from among the animals that came before him in procession. God asked, "What about this one?" And Adam said, "Not on your life." "What about this one?" "Nope." Then God decided to do something quite drastic. He put Adam to sleep and produced that delectable creature Eve. When Adam awoke and saw her he exclaimed, "Wow, that's what the doctor ordered."

God had noted that it was not good for man to be alone, thereby declaring that we are made for community, for fellowship, for family, that we can be human only through associating with other humans; that we do not know how to think, or speak, or behave as human beings except as we learn it from other human beings. In Africa we say a person is a person through other persons. God has made us creatures that are made for interdependence. A self-sufficient human being is subhuman. I have gifts that you do not have, so, consequently, I am unique—you have gifts that I do not have, so you are unique. God has made us so that we will need each other.

We are made for a delicate network of interdependence. We see it on a macro level. Not even the most powerful nations in the world can be self-sufficient. They are forever almost obsessively concerned about their balance of payments situation, which reflects the relationship of trade between nations. It is not good for a nation to be alone. It is not good for a nation to have a large deficit situation, and it is not good for a nation to have too large a credit balance, because it tends to throw the global trade situation out of kilter.

God would have us understand that his dream was of a world in which his creatures, human, animal, and vegetable, would exist in harmony, treating one another as those who had inalienable rights— the vegetable providing food for the animal creation, which, in turn, through its life cycle, would help to fertilize the Earth that nurtured the vegetation; and man and woman would tend the soil and the rivers and the atmosphere in a manner that would be consonant with God's intention, for they were created to have dominion over all creation as God's stewards and representatives. Their dominion was meant to be like God's dominion, caring and compassionate, with a deep reverence for each creature in a way that was appropriate to its nature.

God intended for us to live in the harmony that was pictured as the idyllic existence in a garden. We were to be a happy fellowship, caring for one another, especially for the weak and those unable to care for themselves, valuing persons above things, as those whose worth was infinite and immeasurable. We were meant to care for the whole of creation and offer to God our worship and adoration as rational beings acting as the high priests of a creation that, by being true to its nature, would glorify God. We were meant in a sense to have had the reverence of a Saint Francis of Assisi, who saw the entire universe as peopled by creatures who were members of his family, and so he could speak of Mother Earth, Sister Moon, Brother Sun and could converse with the birds and tame wild animals. It all seems so utopian. The trouble is we took a wrong turn, and our relationship with God went awry. We became disintegrated personalities. We found a wrong center for our egos. We became self-centered and selfish instead of being concerned for the good of others.

We thus broke the fundamental law of our being and things went disastrously wrong. You see, when God gave us the command to have dominion over all that he had created, he intended us to use all the faculties with which he had endowed us. He wanted us to investigate the universe and to discover all the fascinating truths and secrets hidden in this mysterious and beautiful creation. This included discovering awful truths, such as nuclear fission. God created us to be persons who were to be moral agents. Moral responsibility is nonsense where there is no freedom to choose this rather than that course of action, where there is no freedom to choose to obey or not to obey. God took the awesome risk of giving us space to be free to be human.

MAN'S USE OF FREEDOM

God could not have, without contradicting his nature, stepped in to prevent us from using our knowledge to destroy rather than to build. Paul Evodkimov puts it this way, "God can do everything except force us to love Him." He would only look on as we proceeded to create our hell of selfishness, alienation, suspicion, and hatred. He paid the price, so we Christians believe, to try to redress the balance in the gift of Jesus Christ. His creation became fundamentally flawed. Things were out of joint. And so we see the awful spectacle of the arms race where obscene amounts of money are spent on instruments of death and destruction. You know the horrendous statistics. The former Secretary-General of the United Nations points out the following in the foreword to *The Gaia Peace Atlas:*

> At present, almost a thousand billion dollars are expended each year on arms and armed forces, making substantial resources unavailable for sustainable economic and social development. The arms race inhibits confi-

dence-building among States. Instead of providing security, it promotes fear and mistrust. Instead of creating an atmosphere of openness and co-operation, it promotes secrecy and confrontation. And instead of assuring stability, it establishes a precarious balance which is upset by every development in military technology.

The wanton extravagance entailed by the arms race is apparent from the fact that its expense exceeds the total income of the poorer half of humanity and the combined gross national products of large countries in Asia and Africa. The cost is not financial alone. Half a million scientists are employed on weapons research and military projects, when their knowledge and talent could be enlisted to far better effect in the pursuit of life-related goals.

Nor is it just the industrialized countries that indulge in such massive waste. Over the past two decades developing countries have spent more than $200 billion on weaponry, and in some of those countries, military outlays exceed public expenditures on education and health combined. Over and above the direct crippling financial burden, weapons purchases add to the external debt of these countries and create a secondary demand for imports that in turn aggravates their dependence.

The damage to the natural environment as a result of the arms race is also serious and, at times, irreparable. How utterly senseless it is that precious non-renewable resources should be used to build weapons that may destroy more of those resources if they are ever used.[1]

Here are two more important quotations from *The Gaia Peace Atlas:*

Each year, the world spends more on military "security" than the poorer half of humanity earns. The true cost is the loss to all other sectors of human need, a loss compounded over years of neglect. One billion people in developing countries, one in five of world population, live in absolute poverty. Another billion are also inadequately housed and 100 million have no shelter at all.

Three out of five governments spend more on military "defence" than on defence against all the enemies of good health. Meantime, 20% of infants born in developing countries fail to live to their fifth birthday. Unnecessary deaths of infants total nearly 15 million a year—40,000 every day. Four million die from 6 cheaply immunizable diseases, five million from diarrhea preventable by oral re-hydration salts costing virtually nothing. Government in-action and poverty drive on environmental destruction. Failure to take preventative measures in Africa allowed a famine that put 35 million people at risk in the mid-1980s. Each year, 6 million hectares of productive dryland turn to desert; each year, 11 million hectares of forest are de-stroyed.[2]

But what we face now could put these Dark Ages to shame. We live under an ever-growing threat of nuclear holocaust. Unless the nuclear arms race is soon brought under control, it is hard to see how a nuclear world war can be avoided. The explosive power of the nuclear arse-nals is equivalent to well over a million Hiroshimas. If these weapons are ever used in war, civilization would be pushed back to the Stone Age in a flash. Nuclear winter followed by famine, radiation and disease would decimate the survivors.[3]

A minute fraction of what nations spend on their budgets of death would be enough to ensure that children everywhere had adequate housing, a clean supply of water, adequate health facilities, and proper education. People would live with a sense of fulfillment and not labor under a stressful anxiety that is caused by the uncertainties of what the future holds. Many, especially young people, ask whether life is worth living when it is lived under the shadow of the mushroom cloud. Young people are often quite scathing of their elders saying, "Don't tell us about moral values. Look at the state of the world. You have got into two World Wars and many other regional conflicts. We are on the brink of an ecological disaster that is largely due to human cupidity and stupidity. You would have thought with all the technological know-how at your disposal you would have been able to feed the hungry of the world. Instead, with your unfeeling materialism, you have gone on in the affluent North, riding roughshod over your weaker and poorer brethren. Oh, come off it." Who can blame these youth for their nihilism and fatalistic tendencies, when they have tended to be inveigled by the drug culture, transient relations, casual sex, etc. We adults are to blame for the cynicism that sits so oddly on young shoulders.

And yet that, mercifully, is not the whole story. It is remarkable how these very selfsame youths are quick to recognize an authentic person, for they abhor humbug. They recognize goodness and are attracted to it and are ready to pay their due respect to it. They are ready to salute people such as Mother Teresa, and it was largely young people who have saluted that great man from South Africa, Nelson Mandela. I had the wonderful privilege of addressing a mammoth gathering of one-quarter million people at Hyde Park in London in July 1988 when we celebrated Nelson Mandela's seventieth birthday. Most of those present were young people, many of whom were not born when Nelson first went to prison about twenty-five years earlier. Some of them had walked in a pilgrimage from as far away as Scotland. They jam-packed Wembley Stadium for a super birthday concert. They paid this tribute, which was to be repeated when Nelson was released from prison. He received a tumultuous welcome at the same venue. You cannot hoodwink them for too long, they have their heroes, and, in this case, it is a hero without substantial feet of clay.

YOUNG PEOPLE WORK FOR HUMANITY

In addition many of these young people, browned off with what they regard as the self-serving materialism of their parents, have often offered their services selflessly to Third World countries, as members of the Peace Corps for instance. They have been staunch members of Green parties concerned about ecological disaster and have been in the vanguard of the peace movement in many countries. They have often been disillusioned with their parents' generation, but they have not quite given up on the world and on humanity. Here, in the United

States, they were deeply involved with the civil rights movement, and they were passionate in their opposition to U.S. involvement in Vietnam. I can testify to their quite remarkable participation in the anti-apartheid movement.

You could have dismissed their concern for the Vietnam War as in a measure tinged with some selfishness since they were likely to have been due for the draft, and, after all, it was their brothers who were dying in Vietnam. But I must say I was awed when I came to Berkeley once, at a time when the students should justifiably have been concerned about year-end exams and grades, to find thousands sitting in the baking California sun demonstrating against the South African government and calling for their university to divest. I was overawed that they really believed the world could be a better place, that there were some things more important than exams, grades, and degrees. And they were doing it for people some ten thousand miles away. That made me believe in people again.

And these young people, and of course others, helped to change the moral climate in this country so that a Congress that had previously rejected sanctions against South Africa was able to generate enough support for sanctions to have been able to override a presidential veto. Incredible! But it does say that your young people are not just cynics. They are dreamers, and they are idealistic, and they do believe that our world is meant for better things than nuclear annihilation.

We appear to have a nostalgia, a remembrance in our tribal memory, for a different kind of existence than one in which we are living in alienation and hostility. In times, for instance, of major disaster, we become what we are, a global village knowing ourselves to be members of one human family.

We experienced that oneness during the Armenian earthquake. We were aware of the most minute details and out came our compassion and concern, our caring for our sisters and brothers, and this was before the Berlin Wall was breached. The same was true of the San Francisco earthquake. We marvelled at the way the baseball stadium had been built so that the stands swayed but did not collapse, and so with relief we saw thousands preserved, and it was happening as to each of us in whatever part of the globe we lived. When whales were trapped in the Arctic the whole world watched on tenterhooks the saga of their rescue unfolding. Most recently it was not disaster that united us. It was celebration. The whole globe was as one as the world watched the release of one prisoner, Nelson Mandela, from prison after twenty-seven years of incarceration, and it was beautiful as we realized our essential oneness.

Yes, God's dream has been shattered by our greed and our desire for an improper autonomy and independence, which have led to wide-scale alienation and brokenness. In religious terms, our sins have had devastating consequences for God's world. The Genesis story again describes existential truth as we experience it. Adam and Eve quarrel and blame each other for the mess in which they find themselves. They hide themselves from God for his holy presence is unbearable to them, much as the bright sunlight is unbearable to someone who has spent time in the darkness of a cave. There is a hostility between them and the rest of creation so that they will seek to crush the head of the serpent whilst it will pursue them to bruise their heels. The ground that formerly produced all that was necessary to feed the human and animal creatures now brings forth weeds, and work which used to be wholesome is now a drudgery.

In the story of the Tower of Babel human beings are no longer able to communicate since they do not understand one another's languages. Human society has become impossible, and people are separated from each other and scattered on the face of the Earth, forever cursed to be at each others' throats, unable to live for long at peace and harmony with one another, fearful and mistrustful of one another, seeking to find an elusive security in ever increasing arsenals; grabbing as much of the resources of the world for their exclusive use as they can, thereby generating jealousy and resentment in those who have been excluded, breaking up the human community into those who have far too much of the good things of God's world and those who have far too little.

And yet we have caught glimpses of a different way of ordering things. We have on rare occasions shown that it is possible to share, to cross national boundaries, to demonstrate compassion and caring. We have an inner hunger for this other dispensation, which is why we experience a frustration with things as they are. The Bible speaks about this golden age coming, and, strangely, it is described in terms reminiscent of the good times that have passed. The time coming is described by the prophet Isaiah in terms of a paradise regained after paradise had been lost (11 Isaiah).

REALIZING GOD'S DREAM

God's dream may have been shattered, but the pieces can be picked up and put together again. God wants to enlist us in this glorious enterprise of helping him to realize his dream. And the Nuclear Age Peace Foundation is part of that exhilarating enterprise. All people of goodwill must work together to galvanize public opinion to produce the moral climate that will enable governments to say they do not intend to go on improving their standard of living and thereby continuing to use up so much of the world's resources.

We must try to make it politically possible for governments and political parties to remind people that we really belong to a world community, that we are our brother's brother and our sister's sister, and so we have a moral responsibility for them. We should make it possible for political parties to canvass support for manifestos declaring that they want their supporters to live more simply so that others may simply live.

We are reminded in *The Gaia Peace Atlas* that "Human behavior is intimately related to the availability of basic resources. When a shortage of resources threatens life styles or life itself, rivalry for resources leads to aggression, the development of power elites and, ultimately, to war."[4]

Concerns about ecology have now become serious political concerns. Politicians know that more and more they will be judged on their attitude toward the issue of the preservation of nature and its resources. This was not always the case. It is because people lobbied for change that we have reached the present stage. Thus it is possible to change attitudes. We should support the peace movement and all those many organizations that seek to outlaw nuclear war.

Again, *The Gaia Peace Atlas* reminds us: "Peace is inseparable from sustainable living—we cannot have one without the other. Yet we have to get there first. We have to build bridges to the future.

- We must break the link between security and military force, and redefine security. Real security is human and planetary security, common security with all nations.
- We must learn non-violence and conflict resolution.
- We must apply Gaian constraints to decisions.
- We must disarm, halt the arms race and divert our military resources to pressing global problems.
- We must place moral controls on technology, especially military technology, and predict with caution any new technology's consequences: if in doubt, don't!
- We need new attitudes. Tomorrow's citizens must accept that survival depends on commitment to moderated national sovereignty and global loyalties.
- We will have to frame new systems of governance that limit the abuse of power and encourage new leadership.
- We must spread the spiritual revolution that is coming: of concern for nature, justice and peace.
- And we must abolish war. We need no longer enquire why or how. We simply have to stop.
- Many of these 'bridges' demand very difficult decisions for politicians. This will take huge public pressure. Each of us has a choice. Either we give priority to peace and sustainable living, or we will not survive long into the 21st century."[5]

A MORE EQUITABLE WORLD ORDER

We should work for a more equitable world economic and political order and be stalwarts in the struggle for human rights globally.

Julius Nyerere puts it succinctly when he declares, "Abolition of all nuclear weapons is vital for humankind's security. But this is not enough, by itself, to bring peace to the world. War is not caused by weapons; these are simply implements used in war. Real and sustainable peace is therefore not obtained simply by abolishing armaments.

For the basis of war is injustice; and the foundation of real peace is justice and equality.... Peace in the world requires Justice in the world. None of us can escape the responsibility to act for our own future."

Pope Paul VI declared, "If you want peace, work for justice."

We need to be reminded that God has a dream for us in which all his children, and, indeed, the whole of his creation, will live in the harmonious interdependence that was God's intention from the beginning.

Barbara Ward says rightly, "We must live in an absolutely interdependent planet; we must work to bring this about or the bright day will be done and there will be dark."

ONE HUMAN FAMILY

God made us for togetherness, for *koinonia*, for fellowship, for family. He intended us to live in a delicate network of interdependence as members of one family, the human family, God's family.

7 | MAIREAD CORRIGAN MAGUIRE
A Nonviolent Political Agenda for a More Humane World

Sometime ago I was speaking to a professor of psychiatry about world peace. He told me he believed that scientists in the world community know the problems humanity is faced with, such as the environment, poverty, etc., and that in many cases, solutions to these problems already exist. He believed much of the intellectual analysis has been done on these problems and what is needed now is to be able to touch people's hearts and to create the confidence and collective will of the people of the world to change things.

I am convinced there is much in what he says. There is a growing world recognition and consensus that war and militarism, environmental problems, poverty, social injustice, human rights violations, and the lack of real democracy are urgent problems facing us all. However these problems can be solved if the "political will" can be created. They can be solved, but it will take much money and the application of our finest minds and talents committed to the challenge. No one country can do the job alone. We need international cooperation. The money can be made available if the will exists in both the people of the world and their governments. I believe the will of ordinary people to do something to deal with these problems already exists, but it is not yet being reflected in the policies of their governments. Many of the world's governments have actually cut military budgets. Yet, we all know that if money was made available from each country's military budget and diverted into the appropriate United Nations' institutions, millions of lives could be saved immediately, and the money could go a long way toward solving other problems.

There is nothing I have said so far that each of us does not, in our hearts, know to be true. So I have to ask myself, "Am I only wasting paper in saying all this?" If so, then there goes another tree to provide me with my paper, a tree for which I am responsible. I know I must take responsibility for every act I do, which in turn affects others and the planet.

TAKING RESPONSIBILITY

Taking responsibility for our own actions may be the greatest contribution we can all make toward solving these problems and is surely part of the process of beginning to create what Martin Luther King, Jr., called "the beloved community." Can you imagine how different things could have been in Hitler's Germany had people taken "personal" responsibility for their actions?

This thought came back to me very strongly when, a few years ago, I made a pilgrimage to the Auschwitz concentration camp in Poland. It was the most horrible place I have ever entered. I walked around weeping, all the while silently asking myself, "How could human beings do this to fellow human beings?"

In one of the gas chambers, a rabbi and a priest led our small group in prayer. During the prayer, local church bells rang out. I asked a companion about the bells. He explained that they were the bells of the local Catholic church for Sunday mass. He went on to say that this torture camp could not have operated without the help of the local Catholics, who presumably serviced and worked in the camps during the week and went to church on Sunday.

I left Auschwitz with the utter conviction that we must uphold human life and rights and each work passionately for justice. We must learn from the horrors of the past—we must not repeat them.

Several years later during a visit to Jerusalem I was deeply saddened to witness firsthand the bitter conflict between the Israeli and Palestinian peoples. I am convinced that the only way forward for the Palestinian and Israeli peoples is one based on a dialogue of trust and respect for each other's human rights and the right of each to their own homeland. To help this process each of us needs to take personal responsibility for its success and to live out the spirit of nonviolence.

When I speak to people about my belief that we need to live out and teach active nonviolence at every level of society, people often ask, "Ah! But what about Hitler?" They are right to ask this question, but it is important to bear in mind that the death of Hitler did not mean the death of fascism. We must remember, too, that Hitler was only one man. It was thousands of people taking on the "spirit" of Hitler, the spirit of hate, cruelty, etc., that made Auschwitz possible. Had each person taken responsibility for their own actions and not merely said, "It was for my country, I was only following orders, etc.," things would have been very different. Of course, some were afraid for themselves and their families, but we must strive to overcome fear with courage and to do what our hearts tell us to be right.

The personal need to inform our conscience, and to do what our conscience tells us to be right, is important for our spiritual and physical wholeness, and for the wholeness of others and of our planet. The making of weapons of destruction, even if one is only very slightly involved in the process, is participating in the death of fellow human beings and the destruction of the environment. These weapons are killing people without ever having been fired since the money involved to build them could be used to feed the hungry.

The nuclear Trident submarines are polluting the seas and destroying the oceans, which we need for our very lives, and putting the safety of all of us daily at risk. Everyone remembers Chernobyl, but it is not generally known that there have been many accidents involving nuclear material in America. Independent critics say there have been 125 fires and explosions at nuclear production sites.[1] Between 1945 and 1980 there were 691 nuclear weapons tests in the United States. In 1963 the nuclear tests went underground. However, underground tests still send fallout by releasing radioactive clouds. According to Colonel Raymond Brim, who for ten years was in charge of monitoring leaks, "Americans were exposed to dangerous levels of radiation from 'safe' underground tests all through the 1960s and 1970s and remain in danger today. Just as the risk of fallout continues so does the conscious government efforts to cover up the situation."[2]

For forty years there existed the illusion that nuclear weapons were a mutual deterrent and provided stability between the United States and the Soviet Union. With the ending of the Cold War many people are lulled into thinking the nuclear danger is over. However, we are now faced with a possibly even greater danger, due to the lack of control in new republics and the spreading of nuclear weapons to smaller nations eager for nuclear technology. (There are four ex-Soviet republics with nuclear weapons and eleven republics with tactical short-range weapons.) Smaller nations will sign the Non-Proliferation Treaty in 1995 only if the big nuclear powers are willing to commit themselves to ending nuclear testing and beginning nuclear disarmament. If the United States does not give a clear lead on this, the Non-Proliferation Treaty will not be renewed, and the nuclear arms race will escalate beyond control.

Some people will try to fool themselves that these nuclear weapons will not be used, but remember Hiroshima and Nagasaki. Remember also that it was not necessary to drop these nuclear bombs in order to end the war. The use of nuclear weapons was also threatened during the Vietnam War.

The late Father George Zabelka, who was a Catholic priest on Tinian Island in 1945 and blessed the crew going out to bomb the cities of Hiroshima and Nagasaki, spent his later life working for world peace. He took personal responsibility for his part in the terrible crime against the Japanese people and returned to Hiroshima and Nagasaki, to ask forgiveness of the *hibakusha* (survivors). Several years ago, during a visit to Japan, I asked the forgiveness of the Japanese for the bombing of Hiroshima and Nagasaki. I believe it is only by saying we are sorry for the wrong we have done that we can move forward in genuine reconciliation and healing.

STOP MAKING WAR RESPECTABLE

Many of us were deeply inspired by the life of Father Zabelka as he walked around the world for peace, with the words "Hiroshima" and "Nagasaki" on each shoe. His message to all was "Stop Making War Respectable." Father Zabelka followed in the footsteps of two other great prophets of nonviolence America has given the world—Martin Luther King, Jr., and Dorothy Day. Their lives inspired millions, as I believe Father Zabelka's life will continue to do even after his death on April 11, 1992. Up until the last days of his life he continued to hand out peace buttons saying, "Do something for peace." In his early life, his army friends nicknamed him "General George," but he will live on in our hearts as our friend who was to us a gentle prophet of nonviolence.

With his words, he reminded us that we must put people above our flags and nationalism and stop glorifying war and violence. We honor those who, in the past, believing it was the only way to resist evil, went to war. But now the human family has a new way, the way of nonviolence. So, in the future, when a dictator or a government takes a country to war, it will be considered a sign of weakness, impatience, and an inability to solve human conflict with imagination and vision. We people of the world need to have international laws that protect us from murderous and barbaric wars often carried out in our names, but without our consent. International laws could be established so the political leaders are held accountable for their war crimes.

It would be nice to speculate that perhaps by the time such legislation comes into place at the United Nations it will already be obsolete, since war itself will have become obsolete. But who would have believed that, following the end of the Cold War and so much progress brought about by the nonviolence of the peoples of the former Eastern Bloc countries, that our leaders could have again taken us backward into the war in the Persian Gulf. That war has left behind such suffering and tragedy. Words do not come to me to describe the barbarism of it all.

No one can be in any doubt today how the weapons of war have developed, from tanks to the use of thermonuclear, chemical, and bacteriological arms. In an article in the Vatican newspaper, in July 1991, tracing the development of warfare from early Christian times (when Christians did not kill and refused to be soldiers, following Christ's commandment to love their enemies) up to present-day weapons of mass destruction, the writer ends by saying, "IT IS NECESSARY TO CONCLUDE THAT MODERN WAR IS ALWAYS IMMORAL."[3] This is a vitally important statement.

Down through history, many Christians have struggled in conscience with a choice between Jesus' nonviolent love of enemies and an allegedly "just war" theory. Father William Johnston, speaking about the "just war" theory, says, "It seems to me that we cannot have peace until we throw the old just war theology out of the window and search for something new based on the gospel."[4]

It seems to me time too for military workers to search their consciences regarding working on death machines and for those who participate in the trafficking of death machines around the world to do the same.

Hitler's Germany could have been very different had individuals taken responsibility for their actions. In his book *Conjectures of a Guilty Bystander*, Thomas Merton quotes the following excerpt from a letter, written by I. A. Topf and Sons, a manufacturer of heating equipment, to the Commandant of Auschwitz, concerning a new heating system:

"We acknowledge the receipt of your order for five triple furnaces, including two electric elevators for raising the corpses and one emergency elevator. For putting the bodies into the furnace, we suggest simply a metal fork moving on cylinders. For transporting the corpses, we suggest using light carts on wheels. We are submitting plans for our perfected cremation ovens, which operate with coal, and have hitherto given you full satisfaction. We guarantee their effectiveness as well as their durability."[5]

It must be remembered that Hitler was one man who required thousands of other people to help him in the genocide of six million Jews. Merton also quotes Heinrich Himmler as saying at Nuremburg: "Most of you know what it means when a hundred corpses are lying side by side, or 500, or 1,000, but to have stuck it out, and at the same time, apart from understandable human weakness, to have remained decent fellows—this is what made us great. Merton's comment? "Decent, indeed, but damned."

I think it is also worth remembering what Thomas Merton wrote in *Faith and Violence* about death and genocide as big business,

The theology of violence must not lose sight of the real problem of violence, which is not the individual with the revolver, but death and genocide as big business. This big business of death is all the more innocent because it involves a long chain of individuals, each of whom feels himself absolved from responsibility. We know, for instance, that Adolf Eichmann and others like him felt no guilt for their share in the extermination of the Jews. This feeling of justification was due partly to their absolute obedience to higher authority, and partly to the care and efficiency which they put into the details of their work. Since they dealt with numbers and not with people, since their job was one of bureaucratic organization, they apparently could easily forget the reality of what they were cooperating in. The real problems of modern war do not occur in the rare instances of hand-to-hand combat. The real problems of modern war occur in the remote planning centers of organized technological destruction. Modern technological mass murder is abstract, corporate, business-like, cool, free of guilt feelings, and therefore a thousand times more deadly and effective than the eruption of individual violence. It is this polite, massively-organized, white-collar murder machine that threatens the world with destruction, and not the violence of a few desperate teenagers in the slums. But our antiquated Christian theology myopically focusses on individual violence and does not see this. Our antiquated moral theology shudders at the phantasm of a mugging or a killing on our doorstep. But it blesses and canonizes the antiseptic violence of corporately-organized murder, because corporate murder is respectable, efficient, clean, and above all, because corporate murder is profitable.[6]

In 1987 Nobel Laureate Professor George Wald wrote,

All kinds of reasons are put forward—military and political, internal and external, involving adversaries and allies. I wish to speak of one that is rarely discussed directly: 'Defense' is an enormous, lucrative and high favored business in the U.S. It employs over three million workers, about a sixth of our entire industrial workforce.

In 1985, procurement by the Department of Defense involved contracts totalling $150.7 billion. That includes all nuclear warhead research, development and production, which is charged to the Department of Energy. In 1985, the McDonald Douglas Corporation, our No. 1 defense contractor, was awarded contracts of $8.9 billion; No. 2 General Dynamics $7.4 billion; No. 3 Rockwell International $6.3 billion; No. 4 General Electric $5.9 billion, and No. 5 Boeing $5.5 billion.

Their profits on Pentagon contracts run to hundreds of millions of dollars annually, yet I, a retired University Professor living on a pension, pay more income tax than they do; for by a special dispensation of the law, they pay none. I believe that a major reason why our government refuses to stop testing nuclear weapons is that it would spoil that business. We have more than enough of the old nuclear weapons, this would stop the development of new weapons. [7]

According to Professor Wald, "an astonishing unanimity on what would need to be done to cool and shortly stop the arms race and prevent nuclear war" already exists among the American people. Why, then, is the democratic will of the people being ignored and their government continuing on a disastrous course of nuclear weapons testing and development?

AMERICA AT A CROSSROADS

Who are these weapons to be used on now that the Cold War has ended? People are crying out for health care, housing, education, jobs. America is at a crossroads, and the choice between military spending or dealing with social and political crises was never more obvious and urgent. If the arms build-up is allowed to rumble on, then it might well be sooner rather than later that people's hopelessness and frustration breaks out in violence. The United Kingdom faced similar problems in its inner cities when, in the face of rising unemployment and poverty, the people were promised a fourth nuclear Trident submarine, bringing the estimated cost of the British Trident System to forty-five billion dollars (twenty-three billion pounds), including running costs. [8]

In a recent address by one of America's best-known educators, Father Theodore Hesburgh, president emeritus of Notre Dame University, to a group of business executives, observed that by the year 2000 one-third of the U.S. minority population will be unemployable because of lack of education. "Give me the two-billion-dollar budget for one Trident submarine and I can turn around the education of minorities in this country."[9]

I have so far been quoting only men, but I would now like to tell about a woman. Many years ago a journalist visiting a home asked the "woman of the house" how she and her husband shared decisions. The wife responded, "Well, he makes all the big decisions, about the real important things, such as politics, world relationships, the Cold War, you know the *big* things. I make the unimportant decisions, like what the children wear, eat, education, health, you know all the *little* things."

Today, the outlook of many women has changed. They know that these "little" things are the really important things. Many women are now playing an equal role in business and political life, and they are setting an urgent nonviolent political agenda to obtain a decent quality of life, based on respect for human beings. They have a wide world vision too, and see the world's children as their own, for whom they are taking responsibility. They know it is bread not bombs that people need; it is Third World debt cancellation not deals that is needed.

These women want neither to dominate the Third World with Trident missiles nor to dehumanize and humiliate them with charity and handouts. Women are working not only for equality for themselves, but for equality for each human person. They expect demilitarization in order to release money for the *important* things in life.

HARD BIRTHING OF A NEW HUMANITY

It may seem to many who have worked so hard for disarmament that it is an impossible task, that we are up against too strong odds to succeed. But I believe if we all unite together as a human family with a common vision of building a polity based on respect for each human person and respect for our environment, then we will see unimaginable changes. I do believe we are on the edge of a quantum leap into a whole new way of organizing and living as a human family. What we are witnessing today is indeed the hard birthing of a new humanity—a whole new way of people relating to each other and a recognition that we humans are not the center of the universe, but rather are a part of it, with rights and responsibilities to build a secure future for ourselves and our children.

We must have no human enemies in this task. Each person is needed for the work. Our very allies are those in the military industries. They too are men and women who in their hearts know that life and the Earth are gifts to be celebrated and rejoiced, not destroyed.

In the past we used the weapons of war and violence because they were all we knew. Now we have the methods of active nonviolence— surely a more civilized and creative way of solving our problems. We must encourage all people of goodwill to join in the work of abolishing war and weapons, not out of fear of dying, but out of the joy of living.

Nonviolence is not just for an elite few, it is for everyone; it is a way of life based on respect for each human person and for the environment. It is also a means of bringing about social and political change and resisting evil without entering into evil. It is a whole new way of thinking. Remember, a gun or a nuclear weapon is of no use if the will to kill does not exist in the mind. It is the very idea in the human mind that we have a right to take another's life that we must begin to change. The choice is "to kill or not to kill," that is, to kill or to live an unarmed life, fully alive, rejoicing and celebrating this gift we have all been given. The choice is up to us.

In trying to decide what to do, when faced with such enormous problems, sometimes we can feel powerless and imagine that we *personally* cannot do anything that will really make a difference. However, I passionately believe that nonviolence is a powerful force that each of us can cultivate in our daily lives and that through the power of love and truth we can each make a difference. America's own prophet of nonviolence, Martin Luther King, Jr., said of this power, "I've decided that I'm going to do battle for my philosophy. You ought to believe something in life, believe that thing so fervently that you will stand up with it till the end of your days. I can't make myself believe that God wants me to hate. I'm tired of violence. And I'm not going to let my oppressor dictate to me what method I must use. We have a power, power that can't be found in Molotov cocktails, but we have a power. Power that cannot be found in bullets and guns, but we have a power. It is a power as old as the insights of Jesus of Nazareth and as modern as the techniques of Mahatma Gandhi." [10]

Let us all use this power together and, as Dr. King urged, "join with the Earth and each other, to bring new life to the land, to restore the waters, to refresh the air, to renew the forests, to care for the plants, to protect the creatures, to celebrate the seas, to rejoice in the sunlight, to sing the song of the stars, to recall our destiny, to renew our spirits, to reinvigorate our bodies, to recreate the human community, to promote justice and peace, to love our children and one another, to join together as many and diverse expressions of one loving mystery, for the healing of the Earth and the renewal of all life." [11]

I wish you peace and joy in your life and pray above all that you take time to be happy.

8 | LARRY AGRAN
A Peace Conversion Program

It used to be that few American mayors dared to speak publicly about foreign policy issues and the damaging effects of military spending. We were told that these were matters of "national security"—off-limits to all Americans except a tiny handful of highly placed federal officials. Fortunately, with the advent of a new generation of urban leaders, things are changing now. Mayors worry about national security too.

But to us, national security means more than weapons—more than Star Wars, MX missiles, and Stealth bombers. To us, national security means strong families and strong neighborhoods in economically vibrant communities. It means rewarding jobs in modern industries that are competitive in the global marketplace. It means health care, education, child care, and transportation worthy of our citizens. It means decent, affordable housing for *every* American. It means safe streets in every part of town, so that people can walk at night without fear. It means clean air and clean water and land free of poisons. In short, national security means cities that are good places to live, in a country that is a good place to live, on a planet that is a good place to live.

THE TYRANNY OF THE ARMS RACE

Measured in these terms, our national security has been breached. Our cities and our people are under siege. Even though the Cold War is over, the enemy we face is a continuing arms race that has, since 1947, consumed $10 trillion in American wealth—a figure that defies comprehension. Beginning with President Truman—and led and supported by every president and every Congress since—our national politicians have built the kind of military-industrial complex that President Eisenhower warned us against. In the process they have relentlessly drained our cities of the tax dollars and the intellectual resources essential to urban, national, and global progress.

Once thought affordable, even desirable, as an economic stimulus, here is what the wretched arms race has come to: Driven by nuclear weapons testing and development, America's share of the $900 billion spent each year on the global arms race is still $300 billion. The true price of our twisted federal priorities is painfully evident in our cities and towns, where our streets and bridges crumble; where our factories rust; where our schoolchildren remain mired in ignorance; where displaced farm families seek refuge; and where drug addiction, violence, homelessness, hunger, and poverty are on the rise. What we see in our cities is, in fact, what is going on globally: Our economic systems, our social systems, and our ecosystems are bending and even breaking under the burden of an arms race that is nothing short of tyranny.

A THREE-POINT PROGRAM

Faced with the tyranny of the arms race, some of us have not hesitated to call for radical change, for revolutionary change, for a fundamental reordering of our public priorities. What, then, is the new order of things that we seek? We seek to bring about what we call "peace conversion," and our program consists of three essential elements. The first element is genuine disarmament—not simply arms control agreements that, in effect, lock in massive weapons expenditures, but deep cuts in both nuclear and conventional forces. Preferably, these are to be achieved as multilateral agreements with Russia and other nuclear powers. But even in the absence of comprehensive international accords, it is in our self-interest to restructure our largely offensive military forces into truly defensive forces, permitting enormous annual savings of up to $200 billion, while actually enhancing global security and our own national security.

The second element of our peace conversion program is to capitalize on the massive liberation of resources associated with superpower disarmament to achieve urgent domestic goals, such as an end to further federal debt accumulation and swift victories over homelessness, hunger, poverty, and pervasive environmental degradation.

The third element of our program is to apply some of the liberated resources—at least $40 billion per year—to address the global environmental emergency we face, including global warming, ozone depletion, and the related problems of Third World debt, Third World impoverishment, and population growth.

If you're inclined to say that "peace conversion" is a nice idea but an unrealistic one, I ask you to reconsider. Isn't the plain truth just the opposite? It seems to me that the course we're on now—pursuing a disastrous arms race years after the Cold War has ended—is what's totally unrealistic. We simply cannot go on like this. I say this as a citizen, but also as a practical politician who is experienced in the nuts-and-bolts realities of governing a community. It's not really very complicated. We know what it takes to run a decent city. We know what it costs to secure a livable environment. We know that if you spend money on all the wrong things, you won't have what it takes to do the right things. That's what budgets are all about. And that's why I want to describe to you the sort of post-Cold War peace conversion budget that I first proposed to the Budget Committee of the U.S. House of Representatives in 1987.

A BUDGET FOR "DEFENSIVE DEFENSE"

In my testimony to the House Budget Committee, I said that the continuing burden of a bloated military budget was, in fact, ruining America and ruining our planet, and that the most urgent task before the country was to cut the $300-billion military budget by at least half.

I told the committee how it could be done, pointing to four areas rich in cost-cutting potential. First, I said, let's do what everyone but the military contractors and some corrupt members of Congress agree must be done—let's eliminate the flagrant waste, fraud, and abuse that infects the entire weapons procurement system. The savings: $30 billion to $50 billion per year. That's not my estimate. It was David Stockman, President Reagan's first director of the Office of Management and Budget, who asserted as early as 1981 that the Pentagon was awash in fraud and abuse, accounting for as much as $30 billion each year. More recently, Robert Costello, the Pentagon's director of procurement, noted that 30 percent of the Pentagon's $150-billion procurement budget is wasted every year. How do you eliminate waste, fraud, and abuse of such magnitude? You do it the way we do it with any program at city hall that is out of control. We take away the money, we fire the rotten managers, and we replace them with new managers whose success is measured not by the size of their bloated budgets but by their ability to do more with a lot less.

Second, I told the House Budget Committee that the time is here—in fact it arrived long ago—to get rid of offensive weapons and doctrines. The idea that we deter a nuclear power by our ability to launch a first-strike nuclear attack is just plain stupid. We curb the appetite of a potential aggressor by communicating our resolve to *defend* rather than to attack. This means our tax dollars devoted to armaments should be spent primarily on defensive weapons—weapons that will repel an attack, such as antitank and anti-aircraft equipment and short-range jet fighters. These weapons provide real defense and do so at a tiny fraction of what offensive weapons cost. A truly defensive strategy would, at last, allow us to erase a host of costly and obviously offensive weapons programs: the multibillion dollar MX missile, with its idiotic railroad car basing scheme; nuclear aircraft carriers, each costing billions to build and billions more to operate; B-2 or Stealth bombers, produced at a cost of more than $1 billion each and likely to be as useless as their predecessors, the B-1 bombers, which cost a total of $28 billion; the Trident II/D-5 submarine, a $100-billion investment in shameless first-strike overkill; and, of course, Star Wars, which is truly the Strategic *Offensive* Initiative, now costing us at least $5 billion per year, with an ultimate price tag that may reach $1 trillion before the pseudoscientists obsessed with this fantasy ever admit that erecting a shield against nuclear weapons is impossible.

Third, I told the House Budget Committee that it is time to completely rethink and revamp our military alliances. The North Atlantic Treaty Organization is now over forty years old. If a Soviet invasion of Western Europe was ever a realistic threat, the collapse of Communism and the dissolution of the Soviet Union has obviously reduced the probability of major military confrontation in Europe to near zero. If this is so, why are we continuing to spend $150 billion per year on the militarization of Western Europe? Amazingly, U.S. taxpayers, the majority of whom live in decaying cities and towns, continue to fund two-thirds of all NATO costs. This means the average American family is taxed $2000 per year to support the NATO countries, whose aggregate population and wealth exceed our own. Let me put it simply: No one has a greater interest in the security of Europe than the Europeans themselves. It's time they assume full responsibility for their own defense. Accordingly, it's time for us to phase down our annual support of NATO to no more than $30 billion, saving us some $120 billion per year.

Similarly, it's time for Japan and South Korea to pay the costs of their own defense—costs that have been running us at least $25 billion per year. And in the Persian Gulf, we spend $50 billion per year for huge naval armadas and a series of difficult and dangerous missions that, at their bottom line, are simply intended to maintain access to Mideast oil reserves. The answer to all this is to end, once and for all, our dependence on foreign oil through the imposition of an oil import fee that will, to a certainty, produce both revenue and conservation measures that will assure our energy security and free us of the need to risk war abroad in order to stay warm at home.

Fourth, and finally, I told the committee that we must get serious about banishing nuclear weapons. Let's accept the Russian and the French standing offers to stop nuclear testing right now. Let's negotiate even deeper nuclear arms cuts than President Bush and President Yeltsin recently announced. Let's recognize what war planners acknowledged decades ago—that five hundred nuclear bombs, not the tens of thousand we and the Russians possess, are more than enough to meet the requirements of any credible theory of mutual nuclear deterrence.

As for the building of yet more nuclear bombs, no mayor and no citizen who cares at all about protecting the public health and safety can possibly condone this kind of continuing madness. As the *New York Times* reported several years ago in dozens of front-page stories, the government's bomb-builders have knowingly and secretly poisoned the air, water, and land of entire communities with radioactive waste, the lethal properties of which persist for up to 240,000 years, some fifty times the span of all recorded human history. Those who seriously suggest we ought to spend tens of billions of dollars to re-open and keep open bomb factories in South Carolina, Texas, Ohio, Colorado, and Washington, must be truly insane.

Admittedly, to younger Americans who have known Cold War for most of their lives, getting rid of nearly all nuclear weapons and offensive weapons, making our allies pay their own way, and pulling the plug on criminal military contractors may sound like a radical course. Certainly, the budgetary impacts of such policies are radically different and radically beneficial—saving us at least $150 to $200 billion per year in military outlays. Instead of a wildly excessive *military* budget of $300 billion per year, we would finally have an honest-to-God *defense* budget of approximately $100 billion per year. That's more than ample to protect the lives and property of the American people—just as the Constitution requires; but it's not enough to get us involved in undeclared wars in places like Korea, Vietnam, the Caribbean, and Central America—just as the Constitution forbids.

In point of fact, what I am proposing here is what thoughtful military analysts are calling "defensive defense" or Common Security. And it is precisely what President Franklin Roosevelt had in mind in 1941 when, in his famous Four Freedoms speech, he defined the Fourth Freedom as "freedom from fear—which," he said, "translated into world terms, means a worldwide reduction of armaments to such a point and in such a thorough fashion that no nation will be in a position to commit an act of physical aggression against any neighbor—anywhere in the world."

REALLOCATING OUR RESOURCES

Nearly fifty years after President Roosevelt articulated this Fourth Freedom, isn't it time we secured its benefits for ourselves and all humankind? As I often used to ask my fellow mayors to do, take a few minutes to imagine what it would mean if we actually achieved a post-Cold War peace conversion budget, with $200 billion per year liberated for purposes of social uplift. For the record, speaking as one former mayor, here is what I would do with these resources.

First, I would set aside approximately $15 billion per year for what I call a "Defense Worker's Bill of Rights"—to ensure that those civilians who have worked in weapons factories for years are provided a guarantee of income, alternative employment opportunities, and whatever education and retraining may be necessary. We want no victims of the post-Cold War peace we envision. We want all Americans to be winners.

Second, I would urge that we invest $50 billion per year to complete our social security program—making it a truly comprehensive social security plan that guarantees to each and every American income security, health security, housing security, and nutrition security. Today, nearly thirty-five million Americans are officially impoverished. Poverty is smothering thirteen million kids; one in every five newborns is poor, two in five if they're black. As many as three million Americans are homeless; tens of millions are without adequate medical care. It is absolutely immoral that all this human suffering is permitted to continue in a $6 trillion economy—a national economy of unprecedented aggregate abundance. The slogan of every citizen should be "No more needless suffering!"

Third, as a former mayor familiar with the wonderful work that can be done with adequate resources at the local level, I would urge the reactivation and enlargement of the General Revenue Sharing program, this time making $20 billion to $25 billion available annually to the cities and towns of America to rebuild transit systems and libraries, to provide parks and recreation opportunities, and to improve police, fire, and emergency services to make our streets and our communities safe once again. Along with America's millions of current and former local elected officials, I say to the president and to the Congress: Restore our resources, and we'll do the job! Give us back our dollars and we'll once again make America's cities repositories of civilization, culture, and progress.

Fourth, I would heed the recommendation of the U.S. Conference of Mayors that $15 billion per year be invested in federal aid to education. This amount would permit school districts across America to hire 400,000 additional teachers, teachers' aides, and support staff. Class sizes could be cut 10 percent. And both teachers and students alike would be given the fighting chance they deserve to make our education system work again.

Fifth, I would insist that an added $40 billion per year be set aside to meet the global environmental and developmental emergencies we face. The list of environmental horrors is well known—drought and planetary warming, record ozone levels on the streets of our cities, a huge hole in the stratospheric ozone layer, medical waste washing ashore, toxic waste oozing out of the ground, acid rain, dying lakes, diminishing rain forests. Who now can doubt that the Earth itself is seriously wounded? Step by step, working with other countries and working through the United Nations, we must heal and restore the Earth. There is no other way. Also, in an act of humility and common sense, we must invest the billions it requires to restrain the growth of our own species, adopting noncoercive but comprehensive and effective birth control policies.

According to the Worldwatch Institute's Lester Brown and Edward Wolf, to put our global community on a path of sustainable development, it will cost an average of $150 billion per year over the next five years. With the fair-share contributions of other nations and the steady application of these resources through the year 2000, we would be able to protect the topsoil on croplands, reforest the Earth, dramatically slow population growth, become energy efficient and develop renewable energy, and retire Third World debt.

Julius Nyerere, the distinguished former president of Tanzania, spoke on behalf of the poor of the world when he asked: "Must we starve our children to pay our debts?" As Americans, our answer to hundreds of millions of suffering children, and their desperate parents, must be clear and unequivocal. No, we will no longer permit forty thousand children to die of starvation and malnutrition each day. We will, instead, hammer our swords into ploughshares, and we will, at last, begin to redeem the future for our planet. If we seize the Cold War's end and immediately free ourselves of expensive arms spending, we will surely reach these goals. Without an end to the continuing arms race, we will surely fail.

Sixth, and last, the kind of post-Cold War peace conversion budget

I am talking about is so rich in liberated resources that we can do more than overcome decades of social neglect; we can do more than restart the entire world on a path toward sustainable development; we can also sharply reduce the annual federal budget deficits that threaten to impoverish future generations.

So there you have it—a post-Cold War agenda for America: a genuine structure of defense to accompany substantial military disarmament and a budget we can live with, indeed, a federal budget that will usher in a revolution of productive priorities at every level of society—local, national, and global.

CONFRONTING THE MORAL CRISIS OF MILITARISM

Isn't this a future worth struggling to achieve? If it is—if you agree that the case for fundamentally changed priorities is a powerful one—the question then logically arises: How do we get there from here? How do we achieve a post-Cold War peace conversion budget? The answer, I think, is that we who say we wish to lead—America's politicians, educators, and citizen-activists—must over and over again speak the truth about what we see. And the truth is that we cannot possibly do our jobs to provide for the health, welfare, and safety of our citizens under the tyranny of current federal priorities.

But simply speaking this fundamental truth is not enough. We must challenge each and every American with this truth. I have learned from experience that political speeches, pronouncements, and press conferences are not enough, on their own, to change things. I believe as leaders we must go further and actually challenge citizens to choose what kind of city, what kind of country, and what kind of world they want. As Americans, the vast majority of us are good at making choices provided we have real choices to make. That is what democratic self-government is all about.

As the former mayor of a militarily dependent community, I used to ask the citizens who elected me to look beyond our share of the $3 billion in prime military contracts that came to Orange County each year. I asked them to consider the choices. "What's more important for America and for the world," I asked, "maintaining a Rapid Deployment Force of doubtful military value, or building rapid transit systems and other energy-efficient transportation improvements that will allow us to overcome our worst-in-the-nation traffic problems while reducing our demand for fossil fuels?"

What's more important? Producing more nerve gas, more weapon-grade plutonium, and more hydrogen bombs—at a cost of more than $10 billion per year? Or reforesting the Earth at half the annual cost?

What's more important? Building Stealth bombers? Or channeling their multibillion-dollar costs into a trust fund to develop renewable energy resources?

What's more important? Pouring $5 billion per year into Star Wars research? Or using that same amount of money to provide comprehensive family planning services, not just in America, but worldwide?

These are not abstract questions. What's at stake here is nothing less than the moral basis for governance in the late twentieth century. A generation ago, Dr. Martin Luther King, Jr., put it this way: "A nation that continues year after year to spend more on military defense than on programs of social uplift is approaching spiritual death." Dr. King understood that Americans had to make a moral choice because America was—and is—in moral crisis. The moral crisis we face—a continuing militarism that destroys us spiritually just as it bankrupts us financially—is a crisis every bit as acute as the tyranny that caused the American independence movement of the eighteenth century; or the enslavement of African Americans that caused the abolitionist movement of the nineteenth century; or the outrage of segregation that caused the civil rights movement of the twentieth century.

The moral crisis of militarism cannot be resolved by compromise any more than colonialism, slavery, and segregation were susceptible to compromise. We cannot compromise with the Cold Warriors who still hold the Republican party in their grip. Nor can we compromise with the congressional Democrats—many of whom are self-described liberals who say they agree with our goals, but who counsel caution in cutting the Pentagon budget for fear that the Democratic party be perceived as "weak on defense." Never mind that a Democratic party still endorsing Cold War military budgets is weak on urban policy, weak on education, weak on health, weak on environmental protection; it's just plain weak on everything that counts.

We must reject suggestions from any quarter that we be content with a "leveling off" of the military budget at $300 billion per year, or perhaps achieving a $1 billion or $2 billion cut here or there. This is what Dr. King called the "tranquilizing drug of gradualism"—and we should have none of it.

Who, then, are our friends in this matter of reordering national priorities? There are many. We have some in Congress, especially within the Black Caucus, whose members have developed a series of detailed alternative military budgets that cut well over $50 billion in the first year. Outside of Congress, we have friends by the thousands who are mayors and city council members and school trustees—all unafraid as local elected officials to take a stand *against* mindless military spending and *for* progressive social, economic, and environmental policies. And most important, we count among our friends the majority of Americans who are ready for a dramatic change of course. They are ready because they know it is time. Deep in their hearts they know it is time to forever end hunger, homelessness, poverty, and environmental degradation—not just in America but throughout the world. And they sense that all this is possible if we acknowledge and welcome the new global reality: the Cold War is over, and a historic opportunity is at hand to sweep its debris aside, build America anew, restore the Earth, and rediscover the power and the majesty of democratic self-government.

9 | CHANDLER DAVIS
Science for Good
or Ill

Science, seen from the outside, may seem like a free lunch: a source of unexpected wealth and cures for what ails us. Or it may seem like a dangerous juggernaut, generating appalling weapons out of control. From the inside, to those of us who practice it, science as a whole is scarcely visible; it is simply there as the context for our lives. Only with a special effort can we ask ourselves the big questions about the nature of science.

Clearly, both of the simple outsider's views are right. Science can be both beneficial and dangerous. Those who practice science should admit, however reluctantly, that our work can have consequences with huge moral implications, which we are not being invited to control. I am one of those who cannot duck the social responsibility of my profession. We recall that the defendants in the Nuremberg War Crimes Trials were not exonerated on the plea that they were only following orders, and we feel in the same way that we cannot evade the moral issue on the grounds that we only follow where science leads.

Let me give a few examples of efforts by scientists to move toward taking a common moral position. There are many. I will start with one in which I was involved. Hundreds of mathematicians signed a statement that appeared as an ad in the *Notices of the American Mathematical Society* in 1967, right next to recruiting ads from Lockheed, Litton, the National Security Agency, and so on. The statement read:

> Mathematicians: Job opportunities in war work are announced in the *Notices*, in the Society's Employment Register, and elsewhere. We urge you to regard yourselves as responsible for the uses to which your talents are put. We

believe this responsibility forbids putting mathematics in the service of this cruel war.

It is considered quite bad form in our society to blow the whistle on any activity for which money can be paid. By making such a public statement, we put ourselves on the spot. Some of the objections came from outside; some from other scientists. Here are a few of those objections.

OBJECTION #1: "What are you, antiscience? antiprogress? Science is knowledge, knowledge is power. How could you be against knowing more?"

When these critics use the word antiscience, I know what they mean. Hostility to rational knowledge is rife today, and the harmful fallout from technology may feed it. Several centuries ago there was an antiscientific ideology of some importance, even among the learned. People sometimes blamed scientists (in the image of the arrogant Dr. Faustus) for trying to understand things that God did not intend mortal humans to understand. Still I do not see that the call for social responsibility in science is of this nature. I think this objection is, therefore, simply off the subject.

We are not antiscience in general. We do believe that science can lead to an expansion of our understanding, and if the use of science raises problems—of course I *am* saying that it raises problems—we will have to deal with them by understanding them, using *more* knowledge not less.

Those who label anyone antiscientific who questions science are demanding that we give science *carte blanche*. But we must not do this. Science is a human product, and people must control it for human purposes.

A further, more subtle point: there is a hidden bias in this objection. If we exempted science from criticism we would be giving *carte blanche* not just to science in general—something that might be arguable—but to science as it stands! We may agree science is on the whole good, but we must be careful not to suppose it is perfect. Even if every answer scientists think they have now is correct (which is too much to hope), one might still wonder whether scientists have always chosen the best questions to investigate: even true statements may be criticized as trifling or irrelevant.

OBJECTION #2: "You cannot reverse progress. It might have been better not to discover nuclear fission, but you cannot undiscover it."

Well, no, we cannot unlearn what we already know; although, sometimes detailed knowledge is almost completely forgotten. If nations could get their governments to agree that nuclear bomb technology should no longer be used, they might want to stop educating bomb technicians. Practical techniques might become very rusty in one generation. But the principles are very likely to remain available—just as historians who wonder about the crossbow can find enough in the historical and archeological record to build a pretty good working reproduction. And again, we did not suggest undiscovering; criticism of some of science's products does not imply a demand to abolish knowledge.

Still there is something to this objection. The fear of science expressed from ancient legends up to today often includes this warning: you cannot put the djinni back in the bottle; you cannot put the lid back on Pandora's box. True. Our choice of research directions affects what we find now, and moreover, it also affects what knowledge is available to our successors.

OBJECTION #3: "There is no such thing as responsibility in scientific research, because when you do the research you cannot foresee what its uses may be."

This sort of objector points gleefully to the case of Godfrey Harold Hardy. Heartsick to see his fellow mathematicians streaming into war work—I'm talking now about the *first* World War—Hardy became a total pacifist. He declared later in life that he was glad none of his scientific results had ever been of the slightest use to anyone. (A paradoxical stance indeed for this passionate humanitarian: you would think he would have wanted to be of use.) He was ignoring, perhaps because it is mathematically so simple, the Hardy-Weinberg Law, which he contributed to population genetics. He was also ignoring a more spectacular exception, which he did not foresee and which few people could have imagined before the 1940s: the so-called Hardy spaces, whose theory he founded in the 1920s, are now so central to what we call linear systems theory that whole conferences are devoted to them, paid for largely by Air Force grants and attended in considerable part by military researchers.

What do I have to say about Hardy's guilt in the military uses of his ideas? He would have regarded them as entirely deplorable, and on the whole he might have been right. They do not, however, illustrate the impossibility of knowing ahead of time the applications of one's research: granted, Hardy did not foresee any application of these spaces, but *he didn't try*. One of our duties as scientists is to try to perceive the relations between different ideas; it is not a duty we should be reluctant to carry out, because much of the excitement of science comes in the richness of the connections that appear. I think this point is important and too seldom made, but it is only a small part of my answer to this objection.

If Hardy had understood that one of his spaces had potential practical application by way of linear prediction theory, it might have soured *him*, but most of us do not share his extreme rejection of applications. When linear prediction theory was developed in the late 1930s, by Andrei N. Kolmogorov in the Soviet Union and Norbert Wiener in the United States, they did see the connections, from Hardy spaces through probability theory to communication and missile detection. The applicability was intrinsic to their investigation. What is more, they were willing participants in military research against the Nazis. Though they broke relations with the military after World War II—Wiener in a dramatic open letter in the *Atlantic Monthly*—the military did not break relations with their ideas. The djinni was not put back into the bottle.

One can imagine Hardy saying to these two gentle, democratic men, as concerned and humanitarian as he was, "You see, my point is proved. You gave your ideas knowing they had uses, but you couldn't restrict them to nonmilitary uses. When the generals got them, you couldn't restrict the generals to using them only against the Nazis; and they used them for each of your countries against the other." If he happened to notice me, I would come in for sharper reproach because I had the benefit of more hindsight. Some mathematical results I got in the 1970s—after so much had been written on scientific responsibility and after the ad against war work which I just proudly quoted appeared—are also often cited at those same military-supported conferences.

Actually, some of the signers of that 1967 war work ad were simultaneously working on military contracts! Two of them made the newspapers at the time, when the generals threatened to cut off their contract money in reprisal for signing the ad. This outraged many professors as an interference with their freedom of expression. In the end, the threat to cut off their support was not carried out. We might wonder whether these scientists were being consistent. They undoubtedly believed there would be no serious military uses of the research they were doing on weather modification. The military command, however, thought weather modification was a directly military topic, and indeed attempted to turn cloud-seeding into a weapon against the Vietnamese.

OBJECTION #4: "You have no right to censor science anyway. What are scientists? Just the employees who do the work. Decisions on what to do with the results of scientific work are made by society at large; it would be elitist for scientists to claim exclusive rights to the results just because they have this special role of generating the ideas."

This line has annoyed me for years. It bothers me because it is wrong, morally and factually, and at the same time it is so close to right that I hate to have to oppose it.

It is morally wrong, in the first place. If my work, or some part of it, is cruel and anti-human, that touches me more closely than it touches anybody else because I am doing it; it gives me a special responsibility that nobody should try to get me to pass off. This is not an elitist attitude, it applies to every participant in an anti-human project.

The objection is factually wrong, in the second place. Scientists are *not* censoring science or the uses of science, in practice, but others who have less to do with creating it *are*. Let's keep them in mind.

The owners of the Johns Manville Corporation decided to continue marketing asbestos products decades after they knew it was causing thousands of cancers; on a larger scale, the owners of RJR Nabisco (whoever owns it this week) continue to push tobacco decades after they found out it was causing hundreds of thousands of cancers. For a third example, the decision to obliterate Hiroshima and Nagasaki was not made by the scientists (many of them were vocally against it, even Edward Teller), but it was not made by society at large either. The decision was made *secretly* by President Harry Truman and his cabinet, and even long afterward it is hard to get a straight account of their motives.[1]

And yet something about this fourth objection is right. Decisions concerning the allocation of research resources, science education, and the course of technology really ought to be made by society at large. I agree with that. Only this is no argument against my raising the issue of social responsibility in science. Quite the reverse: it is an argument for why we need to talk about it *more*. In this essay, I am going out of my way to raise this issue with nonscientists as well as scientists. If scientists are more intimately involved than the rest, it does not follow that I want to exclude the rest. I do not.

Even if decisions about supporting and using science are concentrated outside the scientific community, we may perhaps legitimately insist on our right to negotiate as a group with our paymasters. When relations with the military came up in the American Mathematical Society in 1987, it was in this form: Hundreds of individual members petitioned for a policy statement (1) calling on the Society to seek more nonmilitary funding for mathematical research, and (2) directing the Society's officers to do nothing to further mathematicians' involvement in the Strategic Defense Initiative. The proposal was submitted to a referendum of the Society's membership in 1988. With over seven thousand voting (about twice the number usually participating in the elections of officers), the statements passed by votes of 4,034 to 2,293 and 5,193 to 1,317 respectively. Now, if only the officers of the society can be brought to act accordingly.

Is it clear that such group stands are legitimate? Or, perhaps, is the only proper form of resistance to the misuse of science an exercise of individual conscience? This is sometimes stated explicitly, as in objection #5 below, but more often it is implied.

OBJECTION #5: "Those of you who do not think you can conscientiously do certain scientific work certainly have a right to freedom of conscience. No need to mount campaigns, just vote with your feet. You can just change your field of science, or even change to nontechnical employment."

Well, sure we can. A lot of us do. John Gofman left his job in nuclear medicine so he could freely publish his own estimates, not his employers', of radiation damage. Robert C. Aldridge quit his job as a missile design engineer so he could publish strategic weapon analyses for all of us to share. Molecular biologists leave the lab to organize agronomical stations for Central American farmers much too poor to pay for them.

Less extreme cases abound: many of my colleagues and students have switched from one "normal" position to another to reduce their involvement with destructive technology or to increase the constructive utility of their work. I mentioned the mathematicians' ad of 1967; one of its signers moved from Lockheed to a university, and another moved from the Sandia Corporation to another university. Recently one of the X-ray laser whizzes left the Lawrence Livermore Labs in search of less bellicose research topics.

And yet, I would not accept the notion that responsibility in science should mean only for some individuals to opt out. That would be an artificial limitation. Nevertheless, our campaigns are often to disseminate individual statements of conscience, and this may have the virtue of clarity. I will give a few more examples of such statements.

An organization called the Committee for Responsible Genetics, led by the MIT biologist Jonathan King, among others, has been circulating this statement internationally:

> We, the undersigned biologists and chemists, oppose the use of our research for military purposes. Rapid advances in biotechnology have catalyzed a growing interest by the military in many countries in chemical and biological weapons and in the possible development of new and novel chemical and biological warfare agents. We are concerned that this may lead to another arms race. We believe that biomedical research should support rather than threaten life. Therefore, WE PLEDGE not to engage knowingly in re-

search and teaching that will further the development of chemical and biological warfare agents.[2]

Bearing in mind the Hippocratic Oath traditionally taken by medical doctors, we might put such statements in broader terms. If physicians state their obligation to use their specialty only for the good of humanity, why not other professions? Consider the following oath proposed at an international conference in Buenos Aires in 1988 by Guillermo Andrés Lemarchand:

> Aware that, in the absence of ethical control, science and its products can damage society and its future, I, . . . , pledge that my own scientific capabilities will never be employed merely for remuneration or prestige or on instruction of employers or political leaders only, but solely on my personal belief and social responsibility—based on my own knowledge and on consideration of the circumstances and the possible consequences of my work—that the scientific or technical research I undertake is truly in the best interest of society and peace.

This statement has been signed, among others, by a large majority of the 1988 graduating class in Buenos Aires, and by many scientists internationally.

The following statement was disseminated at Humboldt State in California in 1987 and subscribed to since then by large contingents at graduations there and at many other universities:

> I, . . . , pledge to thoroughly investigate and take into account the social and environmental consequences of any job opportunity I consider.

A number of prominent scientists have publicly subscribed to the following Hippocratic Oath for Scientists, Engineers, and Technologists:

> I vow to practice my profession with conscience and dignity;
>
> I will strive to apply my skills only with the utmost respect for the well-being of humanity, the earth and all its species;
>
> I will not permit considerations of nationality, politics,

prejudice or material advancement to intervene between
my work and this duty to present and future generations;
I make this Oath solemnly, freely and upon my honour.[3]

What is really meant by such pledges? Is it enough for those who
feel that way to move to a different job?

It is not enough. The reason we raise the issue of social responsibility in scientific societies, many members of which may already be
doing clearly constructive work, and in graduating classes of students,
and in general audiences, is that science and technology are social
products. The technology of Zyklon-B for the Nazis' gas chambers, or
of binary nerve gas for today's weapons, is a product of scientific lore
built up by an intellectual community. The social responsibility of the
biological scientists is not merely to get somebody else's name attached to the job! Just as the Hippocratic Oath should make each doctor repudiate Nazi-style experimentation on human subjects by *all*
doctors, biological responsibility should mean that each biologist re-
frains from misuse of the science and gets *others* to refrain too. Responsibility should be applied collectively.

Unrealistic? Sure. The level of mutuality I am imagining here is
unattainable now. The vision is of a process of deepening a community
code of ethics over many stages. As the need is felt more widely, it can
happen. Right now we see medical ethics being reworked, with great
attention from thousands of specialists. Scientific and engineering
ethics can be developed the same way: publicly and worldwide. So
far, it is lagging way behind.[4]

COMPLEXITY

I have been understating the task. To this point, I have been speaking
as if it were typically easy to see the difference between healthy and
noxious science. As if the only things lacking were goodwill and hon-
esty. No, the big problems are really problematic. The answers are not
clear. And even when hard work makes them clear, there may still be
battles to get the ethical thing done.

Sometimes those of us who are sounding wake-up calls, following
the example of Rachel Carson, give the impression that once we all
wake up the way will be plain. We do that by emphasizing a glaring

incongruity, focusing on it so everyone will see it is serious, at the cost of making it seem simple—whereas, really, its complexity is part of what *makes* it so serious.

Let me try to set the record straight a little by dwelling on how we may try to cope with complexity.

One way to bring order into a confusingly complex problem is to run a "cost-benefit analysis." For example, analysts try to weigh the power to be drawn from the Aswan High Dam or the proposed Sardar Sarovar Dam against the damage caused by flooding of farmland upstream, loss of silting downstream, and destruction of river and sea ecosystems. In the case of British Columbia, they weigh the value of the aluminum smelted with the hydroelectric power against the value of the salmon fisheries destroyed, place dollar values on each item, and add up the balance. More ambitiously, one may calculate the dollar cost of revising power generation methods worldwide so as to restore the carbon dioxide balance (the total cost is in the trillions). Such computations have great potential, but keep in mind their limitations.

First, they are no more precise than the inputs, and it is very hard to know some of the numbers going in. I have never done such a labor of marshalling quantitative data to be synthesized, and I respect the audacity of those who do; my skepticism is not ungenerous to them, I hope; but every user of such analyses can see that skepticism is a necessary part of using them sensibly.

Second, I sometimes insist on asking, *whose* dollars are being considered. The aluminum company owns its refinery and makes a profit. If the analysis shows that the costs outweighed the benefits, does that mean the company owes the salmon-fishing coastal Indians damages for the fish they do not have anymore? If not, why not? If so, then the refinery was a bad investment—or the aluminum was underpriced. (There's a can of worms! If the economic realities are different from what the market saw at the time, then the dollar figures have to be revised throughout.) Similarly, we hear talk of whether "industry" can "afford" to eliminate chlorofluorocarbons. Come now! If the physics of the ozone hole is as now believed, then cost-benefit analysis will show on the contrary that "industry"—that is, the owners of the companies that produce CFCs—cannot afford to produce another *gram* of them. Just let all the billions of people who will lose if the ozone depletion is allowed to continue claim damages, and the alleged profitability of freon refrigerant is sharply reversed.

I had better make it clear—I am not proposing such a lawsuit as a practical course. The suit brought by victims of the Bhopal gas leak showed that the courts are an unreliable agency for correcting this kind of abuse. What I am saying is that the dollars can be added up with a view to exposing it as an abuse. If a corporation appropriated my land to build its factory, this would be recognized as theft in our culture, and its profits would not be sacred but could be used to repay me for my property. If the corporation takes away a people's livelihood or their air, this should be recognized as a crime in a new higher concept of economic justice.

Try applying these elementary notions to all instances of toxic waste. Mines, chemical firms, and nuclear plants operate at a profit and pay dividends, without accounting for the great lakes of poison they spread around them. The wastes are costs of the original production, but they are not charged to those who profited while failing to account for them as costs. Instead, when citizens demand the plants be cleaned up, government taxes the citizens to pay for the clean-up operation—on which the original polluter makes a profit. My favorite example is Hercules Chemical Company of Jacksonville, Arkansas, which drenched the region in dioxin and then formed an organization called "Jacksonville People With Pride" to collect money from the Environmental Protection Agency in a fraudulent sham clean-up. They got away with it for a couple of years. A more serious case is the granting of major contracts for cleaning up military toxic wastes to companies like Hughes Aircraft and General Dynamics, which are listed as major polluters.

Not that I begrudge the chemical and nuclear engineers a job. I positively wish them converted to the clean-up industry, away from the sort of thing some of them have been doing. I am talking about the balance sheet, whose bank account the dollars show in. I could gloss over the point, as some politely do, but that seems to me like becoming an accomplice to fraud.

A third reservation about the cost-benefit analyses is that some things do not *have* dollar values. You may have seen the claim by René Dumont that the present excess of greenhouse gases from modern industrial practices is causing deaths in the tropics, via drought caused by climatic change, at the rate of a million deaths per year. Now, he would not claim much precision in his conclusion, and the chain of inference leading to it is rather long, involving subtle and recent atmospheric physics. His attempted calculation is not absurd, however, and its relevance is evident. My point is just that he was right to present his conclusion as he did and not as a cost-benefit analysis. If the reason for deeming our energy usage destructive is measured in human lives, then by all means let us speak not just of dollars but of human lives.

So often we see scenarios of the same form: A way of life is built around some economic activity, and then unsuspected damage comes to light. Why are we so often caught unaware? If you have the impression there is a pattern here, I think you're right. Greed and opportunism, to be sure. The successful exploiter of resources can defend himself by the riches and the influence got from the very exploitation. I am trying to call attention to another common thread in many of these cases: complexity.

First point: The science of the initial technology is less complex than the counting of its consequences.

The computation of yield from an ore, or of the energy required to raise it and smelt it, is an easier kind of computation than the prediction of the ecological effect of the tailings fifty years later. The interaction of a hundred species at the edge of the desert may determine whether the desert advances into fertile land. Each species can be studied by "clean" science, but their interaction is a "messy" science, ecology.

Messy sciences like geochemistry and sociology tended to be shoved aside in the first centuries of the scientific revolution. Precedence was given to clean sciences because they worked. These days, messy sciences are much studied, perforce; and seeing this, you may get the impression that great advances are being made.

It is true that some big models of complex systems are being run on very fast computers. Some of them even work pretty well; for example, predicting the weather a week ahead is a fairly messy problem that thirty years ago seemed to be intractable but is now fairly successfully handled. Do not confuse this sort of success with understanding. All messy sciences today are poorly understood, some of them much more poorly than meteorology. It is good that some serious and resourceful people like working on them, because they are so important. But if those people are honest, they can endure studying these areas only by having great talent for getting satisfaction out of partial results. "For small blessings give thanks" might be the motto of a worker in messy sciences. You probably remember that the very valuable projections of "Nuclear Winter," which were rightly taken into account by policy-makers (both the powerful and us ordinary citizens), were one-dimensional. They left out most of the known complexities of atmospheric circulation, to say nothing of unknown mechanisms.

But we have to keep doing these rough calculations. Ecology will be a messy science for some time to come. Yet I confess to a bit of un-provable optimism. We may not always be as helpless before messy situations as we are now. Looking at the past fuels my optimism. Three hundred years ago, Newtonian mechanics gave philosophers the feeling that the future could be predicted, but only to the extent that the present was known. It seemed the universe would be understood only by grasping at well-determined causes. Yet probability, which came upon the scene at about the same time, increasingly allowed un-determined causes to become part of understanding too. By the nine-teenth century, they explained thermodynamics as neatly as anything in the deterministic realm, and statistical physics is going on to new triumphs today. In the same way, physics of matter first concentrated on pure crystals because they were neat enough that you could get somewhere with them, and gases because they were simple, and (with the aid of probability) you could get somewhere with them; yet later, glasses and liquids also became manageable. I venture to hope that we will find new ways of thinking about today's messy models, ways as different from the deterministic way and the probabilistic way as they are from each other.

UNCERTAINTY

Here is one more weak point to watch for, as important as any of the others: uncertainty. Criticism of science and technology often hinges on risk. The critic declares the risk unacceptable; the defender insists that the critic is impeding progress. A spectacular instance was—and still is—the guidelines for containing genetically engineered organisms. I am going to use a less prominent example:

The space probe Galileo was launched by a space shuttle. Aboard Galileo was a small plutonium pile. You may have heard the criticism of this plan by Karl Grossman and others.[5] They pointed out that the shuttle launch is not perfectly safe (as sane astronauts like John Glenn knew even before the Challenger exploded), and that if Galileo's nuclear reactor should be shattered during launch it would spray into the atmosphere a quantity of plutonium sufficient to poison millions of people. The planetologists, almost all of them, stuck by the plan.

The launch took place, and the spaceship Galileo went safely on its way; but the issue is still current. In the first place, more than just Galileo is involved. Ulysses has since been launched and other research space vehicles with reactor power are planned.

In the second place, do you know Galileo's planned route to Jupiter? It is not going outward all the way. Rather, it is going step-by-step, picking up a little additional energy in each of a sequence of near encounters with planets. This is an elegant trick. A small object heading toward a planet may brush by either side, getting deflected. Or, of course, it may come in between and crash on the planet. If it brushes by a large planet all alone in space, it will leave with as much energy as it came in with, only its direction will change. On the other hand, in the complicated system of planet and sun, a fly-by can send the small object off with a little *more* energy than it came in with. Galileo is to get such boosts at each of its stepping-stones; and two of these boosts are to come from this planet, Earth. That's right. This little nuclear ship that Karl Grossman was trying to get us to worry about will come heading just about straight at us (remember these fly-bys have to be close near misses if the helpful change in orbit is to take place). Suppose there were a miscalculation? Some miscalculations will just put the spaceship onto a course that will spoil its mission, but some miscalculations will make it become a meteorite. Actually the issue is not primarily miscalculation but loss of control. The steering of the spaceship cannot be corrected if communication with space scientists on Earth is lost, and we know *that* can happen because it did happen with the Soviet mission to Phobos and intermittently with the U.S. Venus probe.

I was saying this to some friends, and they thought I was arguing against the Galileo mission. Not quite so simple. I admit the risk of Galileo crashing into Earth is tiny indeed, and maybe future nuclear-powered spaceships will be a little safer and be launched by a safer booster. I am advancing this example merely as something meriting more thought. It is a good instance of difficult risk evaluation.

Some important scientific experiments—interplanetary probes, genetic engineering—entail small risks of significant damage. How much do we have to want to know something in order to take such risks?

As an old science fiction hand, I am a little on the defensive here. The American science fiction author Ben Bova goes out of his way to enlist us on the side of the nuclear industry: as the space probes' cheering section, he would have us drown out the eco-freaks who want to ground those noble plutonium reactors. There is a resonance from one of my favorite Russian science fiction writers, who is actually two people, Arkadii and Boris Strugatskii. One of their characters in the far future discusses nonhuman extraterrestrial civilizations, the Leonidians, who stagnate because they have achieved union with nature, and the Tagorians, who seem slow to progress because they insist on knowing all the possible bad consequences of their initiatives. We humans, on the other hand, MOVE. But I really must resist the implication that all good old science fiction fans should charge ahead with dubious experiments.

We really do need an analysis of the risks—even when they are small. The basic decision to power Galileo by a nuclear reactor was not the result of such an analysis. The decision was made by the U.S. military, which wants reactors in space because it wants reactors in space. The U.S. military let Ronald Reagan lie on its behalf about what its satellites were going to do up there; it would not be above lying about this. I certainly would not entrust my risk analysis to these people, who have been playing their game of Mutual Assured Destruction for over forty years and would be playing it still if they hadn't found ways to put the survival of the world at even greater risk from their weapons. Safe enough for the generals does not mean safe enough for responsible people.

But suppose we do get together a trustworthy team to do a serious risk analysis, say with the participation of the Natural Resources Defense Council. What should the analysis consist of? A probability computation? But probability theory is regarded as applicable to situations where many repetitions of a random process are made or could be made; expected values can be computed and interpreted clearly provided the gains and the losses from different outcomes are subject to addition and subtraction. Here we do not have such a case. Here we deal with small but unknown probabilities and unknown (perhaps large) penalties. We are in different conceptual territory, that of risk analysis, decision theory, and statistics with small nonrandom samples. This area is like the area of messy sciences: many people are working at it these days; its importance has received well-deserved recognition, but I have to tell you that things are not coming clear. Everything about it is controversial.

Even an Earth-bound example will do; it has been with us for years: if your friendly nuclear power plant next door has a one in a million chance of blowing up within a year in a Chernobyl-like incident is that sufficient reason in itself for closing it down? One in a billion? If you have trouble answering such a question, this does not prove that mathematical education is foundering and you are a generation of innumerates. *Nobody* can answer such a question in a clear-cut way. I am not speaking against the study of decision theory. I am reporting that its present status is pretty primitive. Really, if anything, I am speaking *for* studying it. Just don't hold your breath waiting for definitive answers.

GIVE THE FUTURE A CHANCE

In short, I am calling for fellow scientists to accept their responsibility for the future. I am calling for those who are not scientists by job description to join in the effort. Science and technology are central to the problems I have put forth here, but there is no limitation on who can help solve them. I am trying to communicate my feeling that seeking overall solutions—solutions that will stick—is even harder than the case-by-case solutions we usually think about.

We won't make great improvements in a few years, perhaps. We may have to rely on theories and approaches not yet developed and on co-workers not yet born. That's all right. The future has a right to a share of the action. But only some problems can be left for the future. Any species we allow to die off this decade will not regrow a decade later. The minimum we have to insist on is to leave the next generations a world they can live on—to give the future a chance.[6]

10 | LEON VICKMAN
Why Nuclear Weapons
Are Illegal

Let us assume that we have learned of a planet, Alpha, in a distant galaxy, where intelligent life abounds. We have also learned that Alpha is divided into two major military powers, each of which possesses a weapon so powerful that, if used, would destroy all life for thousands of years. Furthermore, we have learned that the power to use the terrible weapons ultimately resides in the hands of one person in each military domain. Finally, we have learned that the highly developed legal system on Alpha has never rendered an opinion as to the legality or illegality of the weapons, since the courts defer, in matters of military decision making, to the military leaders themselves.

What could be said about such a planet:

1) The living things on Alpha are "crazy."
2) More information is needed to know how this situation came to pass before a value judgment can be stated.
3) Such a situation is understandable and justifiable.
4) The legal system on Alpha needs to be developed further so the issues concerning these weapons can be judicially reviewed.

Obviously, just such considerations trouble many persons on our planet, but it is not as easy to discuss as Alpha's situation, since we have become numbed to the presence of nuclear weapons. Indeed, a majority of the humans on Earth were born after the Hiroshima detonation and know only the world view of nuclear standoff.

Much has been written about the horrors of nuclear war. An estimated 2.2 billion persons could be killed outright by a major nuclear war, according to the World Health Organization.[1] Can any attorney

truly argue that this is not a case for an injunction against such an unbelievable horror?

Surprisingly, until I undertook to bring such a case before a judicial tribunal, not a single lawsuit squarely addressed the issues of the
legality or illegality of the threat of use or actual use of nuclear weapons, and the research, development, production, stockpiling, transporting, and support functions related to such weapons. The result
was exciting. The people of Earth won.

THE PROVISIONAL DISTRICT WORLD COURT

It became clear, after some research, that bringing a lawsuit in a state
or federal court in the United States would not result in a ruling on the
merits, since domestic courts consider such issues as the legality of
nuclear weapons to be "political questions" that require abstention.
Turning to the International Court of Justice in the Hague, under the
United Nations Charter, likewise seemed futile, since defendants in
any suit must agree to the jurisdiction of the court, and only nations
can sue.

How then to do it? It was necessary to search for a court that was
empowered to hear such matters. And it came to pass that such a court
was in a formative stage, within a provisional world government called
the Federation of Earth.[2] Under its constitution, a complete court system could be formed. Upon my urging, a bill was passed at the federation's First Provisional World Parliament in Brighton, England, in
1982, establishing such a court in Los Angeles. The lawsuit was filed
soon thereafter, on behalf of all of the persons of Earth, against
twenty-eight "nuclear" nations. The defendants were divided into
three groups: the superpowers, the nuclear host nations, and the
nuclear-capable nations.

Every step of the process was conducted with meticulous care to
conform to generally accepted legal procedures. The defendant nations were served numerous times with legal pleadings. (India was the
only state to file a responsive pleading, stating it was against the use of
nuclear weapons.) Attorney Gaither Kodis of Bellevue, Washington,
was appointed to serve as an amicus to the court, representing the
viewpoint of the defendants in briefs and oral argument.

PRESTIGIOUS THREE-JUDGE PANEL APPOINTED

During the almost six-year duration of the lawsuit,[3] perhaps the most dramatic event other than the court hearing itself was the appointment of three highly qualified judges to the panel that was to decide the case: Judge Francis A. Boyle, Professor of International Law at the University of Illinois Law School at Champagne; Judge Alfred P. Rubin, Professor of International Law at the School of Law and Diplomacy at Tufts University; and Judge Burns H. Weston, Professor of International Law at the University of Iowa School of Law. The fact that the three judges are leading experts in the field of nuclear weapons law resulted in the three lengthy written opinions by the judges having a far-reaching legal effect. As Judge Boyle stated in his opinion:

> Under article 38(1)(d) of the Statute of the International Court of Justice, this Opinion constitutes a "subsidiary means for the determination of rules of law." It could therefore be relied upon by some future international war crimes tribunal.[4]

The article 38(1)(d)[5] impact of the three opinions cannot be overemphasized, since, as the only legal proceeding on the subject, *In re: More than 50,000 Nuclear Weapons* stands as the seminal case in the field.

Indeed, the three judges saw no impediment to hearing the case, though considerable oral argument was devoted to the question of the power or jurisdiction of the court. When their written opinions were issued on July 1, 1988, they simply stated that: "[T]his tribunal has the necessary jurisdiction," and went on to discuss the merits of the case in three separate opinions.

The primary purpose of this chapter is to examine the views of each of the judges, particularly as to those important holdings in which all three concurred.

INJUNCTION GRANTED; MOST PRESENTLY PLANNED USES OF NUCLEAR WEAPONS FOUND ILLEGAL

The essence of the area of major agreement among the three judges was that each found that the rules of war *do indeed* govern nuclear weapons, and these rules prohibit their use or threat of use under virtually all conditions presently contemplated by the superpowers. To support these holdings, all three judges granted the injunction requested by plaintiffs, prohibiting such use and threat of use of nuclear weapons. Two of the three judges also stated that *planning* for a nuclear war was prohibited.

Initial reactions from the international legal community were quite favorable.[6] It now remains to be seen how the opinions influence military policy of the defendant nuclear nations.

Although a complete analysis of the three opinions is beyond the scope of this chapter, a survey of the highlights of each will be presented, with emphasis on the significant areas of agreement among the judges.

THE BOYLE OPINION

Judge Boyle, in the most responsive opinion for plaintiffs, began by finding that "The atomic bombings of Hiroshima and Nagasaki constituted crimes against humanity and war crimes as defined by the Nuremberg Charter. . . ."[7] He went on to say:

Article 2(4) of the United Nations Charter of 1945 prohibits both the threat and the use of force except in cases of legitimate self-defense as recognized by article 51 thereof. But although the requirement of legitimate self-defense is a necessary precondition for the legality of any threat or use of force, it is certainly not sufficient. For the legality of any threat or use of force must also take into account the customary and conventional international laws of humanitarian armed conflict.

Thereunder, the threat to use nuclear weapons (i.e. nuclear deterrence/terrorism) constitutes ongoing international criminal activity: namely, planning, preparation, solicitation and conspiracy to commit crimes against peace, crimes against humanity, war crimes, genocide, as well as grave breaches of the Four Geneva Conventions of 1949, Additional Protocol I of 1977, the Hague Regulations of 1907, and the International Convention on the

Prevention and Punishment of the Crime of Genocide of 1948, *inter alia*. These are the so-called inchoate crimes that under the Nuremberg Principles constitute international crimes in their own right.

The conclusion is inexorable, therefore, that the design, research, testing, production, manufacture, fabrication, transportation, deployment, installation, maintenance, storing, stockpiling, sale, and purchase as well as the threat to use nuclear weapons together with all their essential accouterments are criminal under well-recognized principles of international law. Thus, those government decision-makers in the nuclear weapons states with command responsibility for their nuclear weapons establishments are today subject to personal criminal responsibility under the Nuremberg Principles for this criminal practice of nuclear deterrence/terrorism that they have daily inflicted upon all states and peoples of the international community.[8]

Judge Boyle went on to examine the broad implications of the existence of nuclear weapons:

When nuclear weapons were first developed and used, there was absolutely no consideration given to the rule of law. Thus, nuclear weapons represent the absolute negation of a rule of law both at home and abroad. The very existence of nuclear weapons requires that the rule of law be subverted both at home and abroad.

Furthermore, nuclear weapons are anti-democratic. There has never been any form of meaningful democratic accountability applied to the U.S. nuclear weapons establishment. The American people as individuals or as a whole have never had any significant input into the process of developing nuclear weapons systems except to the extent that Congress has voted blank checks. The very existence of nuclear weapons systems and their requisite degrees of super-secrecy require that our system of government be stealthily anti-democratic.

Finally, the same is true for the Constitution. Constitutional protections became meaningless when nuclear weapons were integrated into the U.S. foreign affairs and defense establishment. Indeed, the U.S. Constitution has become a farce and a facade in the name of national security as a direct result of nuclear weapons. In a similar manner, fundamental principles of legality, democracy and constitutionality have been trampled under foot by all the nuclear weapons states in their mad stampede toward humankind's nuclear abyss.[9]

After considerable additional analysis, Judge Boyle concluded by stating: "I would grant the injunctive relief as requested in full by plaintiffs."[10]

THE RUBIN OPINION

Judge Rubin, though taking quite a different legal path than Judge Boyle, came to similar conclusions regarding the applicability of the 1907 Hague Regulations:

The most frequently stated arguments concerning the possible illegality of the use of nuclear weapons focus on their asserted cruelty and indiscriminacy. The basic rules are codified in the 1899/1907 Hague Regulations Respecting the Laws and Customs on War on Land:

Article 22: The right of belligerents to adopt means of injuring the enemy is not unlimited.

Article 23: In addition to the prohibitions provided by special Conventions, it is especially forbidden—

a. To employ poison or poisoned weapons;

e. To employ arms, projectiles, or material calculated to cause unnecessary suffering;

g. To destroy or seize the enemy's property, unless such destruction or seizure be imperatively demanded by the necessities of war.

In addition, bombardment "by whatever means" of "towns, villages, dwellings, or buildings which are undefended is prohibited" (article 25) and in bombardments, all necessary steps must be taken to spare, as much as possible, buildings dedicated to religion, art, science, charitable purposes, historic monuments and the like (article 27). This last article has been further refined and expanded. There are about 60 parties to either or both of the 1899 and 1907 Regulations, and the articles noted above are usually considered to codify general international law binding even on non-parties.

Despite its generality, article 22 is fundamental. The notion that the means of injuring an enemy is not unlimited—and the obvious implications that such limits as exist are not merely the technological limits on weapons or the policy interest of a belligerent, but relate to "the right" of belligerents—makes legal analysis necessary for the use of any type of weapon. It may seem to be wise policy to ignore the legal considerations involved in proposals to use nuclear weapons, but any state failing to incorporate those considerations in its actual policies would be placed in potential violation of its commitment to the 1899 and 1907 Hague Conventions or the general humanitarian law they reflect.[11]

Judge Rubin gave to plaintiffs much of what they wanted:

I, therefore, conclude that . . . both the natural law and the positive law contain major restrictions on the use of nuclear weapons; and that to the degree Defendants structure their military postures in disregard of the legal restraints on the use of nuclear weapons, they risk plunging the world into a political and moral chaos for which they will be answerable before a far higher tribunal than this. Recognizing that no amount of monetary damages can compensate for that injury, and that no threat of earthly punishment is available in the international legal order to deter states as such from such actions, and that the war crimes trials the international legal order permits for individuals' violations of the laws and customs of war are unlikely to deter even violations of this magnitude by the force-oriented people whom the political systems of the earth tend to put in positions of authority in most militarily capable states part of the Federation of Earth, I conclude that an injunctive remedy is appropriate. Therefore, I would enjoin action by states and political leaders in planning for, and failing to plan feasible alternatives for, the use of nuclear weapons in all circumstances in which that use, including the threat of that use, is forbidden by public international law as set out herein.

Accordingly, with and to the full extent of the power vested in me as Judge of the Provisional District World Court of the Federation of Earth,

I DECLARE that the international humanitarian rules of war apply to nuclear weapons and their use in warfare, and that they severely restrict the use of such weapons in warfare;

I FURTHER DECLARE that the threat or use of nuclear weapons in ways forbidden by those rules in some cases cannot be compensable or properly the subject of reprisal under them, and that in all cases the threat or use of those weapons in ways forbidden by the international humanitarian rules of warfare is of sufficient interest to the general international community to justify that community in taking legal measures to prevent it.

I FURTHER DECLARE that under the view I take of the international legal order, "police action" and other coercive remedies analogous to the remedies the criminal law makes available to nearly all municipal legal orders, is not available in the absence of an international organization realistically capable of carrying out a law enforcement function; that the United Nations Security Council and other organs of the international legal order are not now able to discharge that function; that under the law of the Federation of Earth, an injunctive remedy is available analogous to the remedies many municipal legal orders give to civil claimants.

I, THEREFORE, GRANT to the Plaintiffs, The People of the Earth, an injunction forbidding the threat or use of nuclear weapons in any way violative of international law, including the international humanitarian rules of war. [12]

THE WESTON OPINION

Concurring with Judges Boyle and Rubin as to the applicability of the 1907 Hague Regulations, Judge Weston delineated six "core rules" of international law regarding nuclear weapons:

first, that it is prohibited to use weapons or tactics that cause unnecessary and/or aggravated devastation and suffering;

second, that it is prohibited to use weapons or tactics that cause indiscriminate harm as between combatants and noncombatant military and civilian personnel;

third, that it is prohibited to effect reprisals that are disproportionate to their antecedent provocation or to legitimate military objectives, or that are disrespectful of persons, institutions, and resources otherwise protected by the laws of war;

fourth, that it is prohibited to use weapons or tactics that cause widespread, long-term, and severe damage to the natural environment;

fifth, that it is prohibited to use weapons or tactics that violate the neutral jurisdiction of non-participating States; and

sixth, that it is prohibited to use asphyxiating, poisonous, or other gases, and all analogous liquids, materials, or devices, including bacteriological methods of warfare.

"Scorched earth" and "saturation bombing" policies, incendiary and V-weapons, and the tendency generally to interpret the laws of war more in favor of the principle of military necessity than that of humanity naturally lead one to wonder about the vitality of these six core rules. However, despite these policies and practices, it still is correct to conclude that the six core rules continue to count as law and that they are understood juridically to apply to nuclear as well as to so-called conventional weapons.

This conclusion is validated, first, in abundant expressions of legal expectation to the effect that nuclear weapons and warfare do not escape the judgment of these humanitarian rules. Indicative of a far-flung community consensus, they include *but are not limited* to the following:

• the unanimous adoption by the United Nations General Assembly, on December 11, 1946, after the advent of the Nuclear Age, of Resolution 95(I), recognizing the principles including the definition of a "war crime" as embracing the "wanton destruction of cities, towns or villages, or devastation not justified by military necessity" and of a "crime against civilian population";

• the negotiation and entry into force of the four 1949 Geneva Conventions on the humane conduct of war four years also *after* the advent of the Nuclear Age;

• United Nations General Assembly resolutions in 1961 and 1972 declaring the use of nuclear weapons to be "a direct violation of the United Nations Charter," "contrary to the rules of international law and to the laws of humanity," "a crime against mankind and civilization," and therefore a matter of "permanent prohibition";

• the dictum in the 1963 *Shimoda Case* (the only known judicial tribunal communication on the subject to date) holding that the bombings of Hiroshima and Nagasaki were contrary to international law in general and to the laws of war in particular;

• resolutions of the International Committee of the Red Cross (which has come to play an important and respected quasi-official role in the implementation as well as the clarification and development of the humanitarian laws of war) such as Resolution XXVIII of 1965 declaring: "The general principles of the law of war apply to nuclear and similar weapons"; and

• the writings of publicists highly qualified in the field.[13]

Judge Weston later made a "common sense" argument:

There is little in the authoritative literature to indicate, either explicitly or implicitly, that nuclear weapons and warfare should *not* be subject to the humanitarian rules of armed conflict. As one highly qualified publicist has put it, emphatically:

"It would be scurrilous to argue that it is still *forbidden* to kill a *single* innocent enemy civilian with a *bayonet*, or wantonly to destroy a single building on enemy territory by *machine-gun* fire—but that it is *legitimate* to kill *millions* of enemy non-combatants and wantonly to destroy entire enemy cities, regions and perhaps countries (including cities, areas or the entire surface of *neutral* States) by *nuclear* weapons.

The world community has in no way consented to the abolition of the humanitarian rules of armed conflict in order to legitimize nuclear war.[14]

Judge Weston summarized his position as follows:

In sum, despite an erosion over the years of legal inhibitions regarding the conduct as well as the initiation of war, there remains even in this thermonuclear age an inherited commitment to standards of humane conduct within which the reasonable belligerent can and must operate. Contrary to the repudiated *Kriegsraison* theory of the German war criminals, which argues that the "necessities of war" override and render inoperative the ordinary laws of war (*Kriegsmanier*), there remains the fundamental principle from which all the laws of war derive, namely, that the right of belligerents to adopt means and methods of warfare is *not* unlimited.

It is of course true that there exists a manifest ambiguity regarding the extent to which the humanitarian rules of armed conflict actually could be enforced in the event of a nuclear exchange. Yet it would be error to conclude that for this reason there is no international law placing nuclear weapons and warfare under their [sic] legal scrutiny. The fact that illegal acts sometimes go unpunished does not necessarily amount either to the acceptance of those acts or to the obliteration of the rule of law declaring them to be illegal. Indeed, if the contrary were true, there would be very little law to point to at any level of social organization.

Furthermore, in view of the horrifying and potentially irreversible devastation of which nuclear weapons are capable, not to mention the very little time their delivery systems allow for rational thought, it is only sensible that all doubts about whether nuclear weapons are subject to the humanitarian rules of armed conflict, as a matter of law, should be answered unequivocally in the affirmative, as a matter of policy. Such a response is mandated, in any event, by a world public order that aspires to the shaping and sharing of values more by persuasion than by coercion; and it is in keeping, too, with the major trends of an evolving planetary civilization, embracing the persistent if uncertain quest for nuclear arms control and disarmament and the accelerating struggle for the realization of fundamental human rights, including the right to life and the emerging right to peace implicitly chartered in Article 28 of the Universal Declaration of Human Rights. Also, it is consistent with the spirit, if not always the letter, of the Nuremberg Charter, the judgment rendered under it, the Convention on the Prevention and Punishment of the Crime of Genocide, and, not least, the Charter of the United Nations itself, together with key General Assembly declarations and resolutions which are widely understood to be the authoritative interpretations of the Charter and, in particular, Article 2(4).

I thus arrive at the conclusion that, while no treaty or treaty provision generally forbids nuclear weapons or warfare per se except in certain essentially isolated or limited circumstances, the conventional and customary laws of war (including the cardinal principle of proportionality that militates between the principles of military necessity and humanity) nevertheless proscribe, at a minimum, any first strike ("strategic," "theater-level," or "tactical") involving either "countervalue" or "counterforce" targeting, any second strike ("strategic," "theater-level," or "tactical") involving "countervalue" targeting, and probably most "strategic" and "theater-level" second strikes involving "counterforce" targeting—that is, almost every standard "strategic," "theater-level," and "tactical" option presently dominating at least Soviet and United States nuclear policy.[15]

I DECLARE that the international humanitarian rules of armed conflict are not obsolete, that they apply to nuclear weapons and warfare, and that they severely restrict the use of such weapons and warfare in almost all instances, especially in relation to the standard "strategic" and "theater-level" options that dominate Soviet and United States nuclear policy;

I THEREFORE GRANT to the Plaintiffs, The People of the Earth, such injunctive relief as they have requested that is consistent with these findings.[16]

THE FAR-REACHING EFFECT OF THE ILLEGALITY OF NUCLEAR WEAPONS

Much as in the film *Amazing Grace and Chuck*, it will only take a few persons to start a peaceful international protest against nuclear weapons that can ultimately impact on the very core of nuclear policy. Remember the pioneering work of Linus Pauling against atmospheric testing, and the crusade of Helen Caldicott against nuclear arsenals. Those who follow can now cite to the authority of the Boyle, Rubin, and Weston opinions. Each person reading these words can pass the message of the illegality to others, and one day those who can press the buttons will refuse to do so, if, for no other reason, out of fear of being tried as war criminals. We are a people of law, a planet of law. We now have the law on the most horrible of weapons. Let us observe it.

11 | FRANCIS A. BOYLE
The Criminality
of Nuclear Weapons

The human race stands on the verge of self-extinction as a species, and with it will die most, if not all, forms of intelligent life on the planet Earth. In the hope of preventing a nuclear Armageddon, the jurists and human rights activists of the world must come together to proclaim certain fundamental principles concerning the requirements of international law with respect to nuclear weapons. It is my hope that the following analysis will serve to define in legal terms the stark dilemma of nuclear extinction that confronts the human race today. It also seeks to establish an antinuclear agenda for other jurists and human rights activists around the world to pursue by applying their unique training, skills, and expertise in a productive and meaningful way toward the progressive yet complete elimination of nuclear weapons from the face of the Earth. Realistically speaking, we cannot expect this to happen in the immediate future. Nevertheless, jurists and human rights activists owe a special obligation to our fellow men and women around the world to struggle toward this goal with all the powers of our professions.

HIROSHIMA AND NAGASAKI

Any attempt to dispel the ideology of nuclearism and its attendant myth propounding the legality of nuclear weapons must directly come to grips with the fact that the Nuclear Age was conceived in the original sins of Hiroshima and Nagasaki on August 6 and 9, 1945. The atomic bombings of Hiroshima and Nagasaki constituted crimes against humanity and war crimes as defined by the Nuremberg Charter of August 8, 1945, and violated several basic provisions of the Regulations annexed to Hague Convention No. IV Respecting the Laws and

Customs of War on Land (1907), the rules of customary international law set forth in the Draft Hague Rules of Air Warfare (1923), and the United States War Department Field Manual 27-10, Rules of Land Warfare (1940). According to this Field Manual and the Nuremberg Principles, all civilian government officials and military officers who ordered or knowingly participated in the atomic bombings of Hiroshima and Nagasaki could have been (and still can be) lawfully punished as war criminals. The start of any progress toward resolving humankind's nuclear predicament must come from the realization that nuclear weapons have never been legitimate instruments of state policy, but rather have always constituted illegitimate instrumentalities of internationally lawless and criminal behavior.

USE OF NUCLEAR WEAPONS

The use of nuclear weapons in combat was, and still is, absolutely prohibited under all circumstances by both conventional and customary international law, e.g., the Nuremberg Principles, the Hague Regulations of 1907, the International Convention on the Prevention and Punishment of the Crime of Genocide of 1948, the Four Geneva Conventions of 1949 and their Additional Protocol I of 1977. In addition, the use of nuclear weapons would also specifically violate several fundamental resolutions of the United Nations General Assembly that have repeatedly condemned the use of nuclear weapons as an international crime. For example, on November 24, 1961, the U.N. General Assembly declared in Resolution 1653 (XVI) that "any State using nuclear or thermonuclear weapons is to be considered as violating the Charter of the United Nations, as acting contrary to the law of humanity, and as committing a crime against mankind and civilization." In Resolution 33/71-B of 14 December 1978 and Resolution 35/152-D of 12 December 1980, the General Assembly again declared that "the use of nuclear weapons would be a violation of the Charter of the United Nations and a crime against humanity." Finally, the International Peace Bureau's Appeal by Lawyers Against Nuclear War (1986)—which has already been endorsed by thousands of lawyers around the world—declared that "the use, for whatever reason, of a nuclear weapon would constitute (a) a violation of international law, (b) a violation of human rights, and (c) a crime against humanity." Under article 38(1)(d) of the Statute of the International Court of Justice, this appeal constitutes a "subsidiary means for the determination of rules of law." It could therefore be relied upon by some future international war crimes tribunal. As jurists and human rights activists, however, our primary concern must be to prevent a nuclear war from ever happening.

NUREMBERG RESPONSIBILITY

As jurists, we are compelled by the Nuremberg Principles to point out the following inescapable conclusions of law to all government decision-makers in the nuclear weapons states: First, according to the Nuremberg Judgment, soldiers would be obliged to disobey egregiously illegal orders with respect to launching and waging a nuclear war. Second, all government officials and military officers who might nevertheless launch or wage a nuclear war would be personally responsible for the commission of crimes against peace, crimes against humanity, war crimes, grave breaches of the Geneva Conventions and Protocol 1, and genocide, among other international crimes. Third, such individuals would not be entitled to the defenses of superior orders, act of state, *tu quoque*, self-defense, etc. Fourth, such individuals could thus be quite legitimately and most severely punished as war criminals, up to and including the imposition of the death penalty, without limitation of time.

THE THREAT TO USE NUCLEAR WEAPONS

Article 2(4) of the United Nations Charter of 1945 prohibits both the threat and the use of force except in cases of legitimate self-defense as recognized by article 51 thereof. But although the requirement of legitimate self-defense is a necessary precondition for the legality of any threat or use of force, it is certainly not sufficient. For the legality of any threat or use of force must also take into account the customary and conventional international laws of humanitarian armed conflict.

Thereunder, the threat to use nuclear weapons (i.e., nuclear deterrence/terrorism) constitutes ongoing international criminal activity: namely, planning, preparation, solicitation and conspiracy to commit crimes against peace, crimes against humanity, war crimes, genocide, as well as grave breaches of the Four Geneva Conventions of 1949, Additional Protocol I of 1977, the Hague Regulations of 1907, and the International Convention on the Prevention and Punishment of the Crime of Genocide of 1948, *inter alia*. These are the so-called inchoate crimes that under the Nuremberg Principles constitute international crimes in their own right.

The conclusion is inexorable, therefore, that the design, research, testing, production, manufacture, fabrication, transportation, deployment, installation, maintenance, storing, stockpiling, sale, and purchase as well as the threat to use nuclear weapons together with all their essential accouterments are criminal under well-recognized principles of international law. Thus, those government decision-makers in the nuclear weapons states with command responsibility for their nuclear weapons establishments are today subject to personal criminal responsibility under the Nuremberg Principles for this criminal practice of nuclear deterrence/terrorism that they have daily inflicted upon all states and peoples of the international community. Here I wish to single out four components of the threat to use nuclear weapons that are especially reprehensible from an international law perspective: counter-ethnic targeting, counter-city targeting, first-strike weapons and contingency plans, and the first-use of nuclear weapons even to repel a conventional attack.

COUNTER-ETHNIC TARGETING

It has been reported that various government officials in some nuclear weapons states have supervised the construction of war plans for the threat and use of nuclear weapons systems that incorporate a philosophy known as "counter-ethnic targeting." In other words, major population centers inhabited primarily by members of certain ethnic groups were selected for repeated and especially severe nuclear destruction because of their constituent ethnicity alone. Whatever the alleged political justification for this practice, all government officials who were involved in the nuclear targeting of ethnic groups as such actually committed the international crime of conspiracy to commit genocide, as recognized by articles 1, 2, 3, and 4 of the 1948 Genocide Convention.

COUNTER-CITY TARGETING

A nuclear attack by one state upon another state's civilian population centers is absolutely prohibited under all circumstances, even if undertaken in retaliation for a prior nuclear attack against the first state's civilian population centers. Consequently, the doctrine of "mutual assured destruction" (MAD) must be abandoned as an element of any strategic nuclear deterrence/terrorist policy currently pursued by the nuclear weapons states. Nevertheless, any plan to substitute for MAD the development of a "protracted nuclear war-fighting" or "war-prevailing" capability is not a licit direction in which to move under international law.

Rather, the correct approach is prescribed by article 6 of the 1968 Treaty on the Non-Proliferation of Nuclear Weapons (NPT), which the United States, the former Soviet Union, and the United Kingdom are strictly bound to obey as parties: "Each of the Parties to the Treaty undertakes to pursue negotiations in good faith on effective measures relating to cessation of the nuclear arms race at an early date and to nuclear disarmament, and on a treaty on general and complete disarmament under strict and effective international control." In regard to the achievement of this latter objective, we must emphasize the continued utility of the U.S.-U.S.S.R. Joint Statement of Agreed Principles for Disarmament Negotiations of September 20, 1961, the so-called McCloy-Zorin Accords.

In the meantime, however, while moving toward the goals set forth in NPT article 6, the nuclear weapons states are obligated to recognize and declare that in the event of a nuclear or conventional attack upon them or the members of their respective alliances, they could not under any circumstances actually use their nuclear weapons against civilian population centers. Although this is already the legal situation, we must call for the nuclear weapons states immediately to conclude an international convention specifically prohibiting both a nuclear attack upon, as well as the strategic nuclear targeting of, civilian population centers. This treaty would then need to be implemented by the nuclear weapons states' respective national parliaments making it a serious criminal offense under domestic law for their government officials or military officers to threaten or plan to use nuclear weapons against civilian population centers.

FIRST-STRIKE WEAPONS AND CONTINGENCY PLANS

A surprise, preemptive nuclear strike by one country against another would be a crime against peace and therefore is absolutely prohibited for any reason whatsoever. Consequently, all first-strike strategic nuclear weapons as well as their concomitant command, control, and communications systems and first-strike contingency plans and practice scenarios are prohibited, illegal, and criminal. In order to strengthen that prohibition, we must call for the nuclear weapons states to conclude a treaty that (1) prohibits the further deployment of first-strike nuclear weapons systems, (2) requires the destruction of those already deployed, and (3) mandates the removal of all first-strike contingency scenarios from governmental war plans.

Pursuant thereto, the nuclear weapons states' respective national parliaments must pass implementing legislation making it a serious criminal offense under domestic law for government officials and military officers to design or practice first-strike scenarios during war games or otherwise. These developments would facilitate the conclusion of an international convention specifically prohibiting the nuclear weapons states from adopting a launch-on-warning nuclear response doctrine as well as all forms of command, control, and communications systems supportive thereof and any forms of testing incidental thereto. Such measures would, hopefully, lessen the likelihood of any nuclear weapons state feeling compelled by the circumstance of a severe international crisis to seriously consider being the first to resort to the use of nuclear weapons.

THE FIRST-USE OF NUCLEAR WEAPONS

The first-use of nuclear weapons to repel a conventional attack would be totally disproportionate and indiscriminate to the threat presented and therefore constitute an impermissible act of self-defense. Therefore, both NATO and the Commonwealth of Independent States must phase out all of their battlefield, short-range, and theater nuclear weapons systems from Europe as part of a mutually negotiated process. In this regard, we must applaud the efforts by the United States and the former Soviet Union to eliminate so-called theater or intermediate-range nuclear weapons systems deployed on that continent by means of the December 1987 INF Treaty. We must also encourage them to initiate negotiations over the elimination of all so-called battlefield nuclear weapons from Europe. The immediate and complete denuclearization of Europe by the respective members of NATO and the former Warsaw Pact states is a political, legal, and moral imperative. In this regard, we must all work together as vigorously as possible to denuclearize the new united State of Germany as soon as possible in order to serve as an example for, as well as a prelude to, the denuclearization of Europe, first, and then the rest of the world.

The former Soviet Union and China have each already given a unilateral pledge of "no-first-use" of nuclear weapons that creates a binding international legal obligation on its own accord. The United States and the concerned NATO members must respond in kind by doing the same and then expressing their readiness to conclude an international convention to that effect. Considerations of international law would fully support such a "no-first-use" treaty as a preliminary step toward the complete denuclearization of Europe. Other nuclear weapons states could then join this convention for the purpose of initiating a denuclearization of their respective regions in the world.

THE CRIMINALITY OF NUCLEAR WEAPONS

As can be determined in part from the preceding analysis, today's nuclear weapons establishments as well as the entire system of nuclear deterrence/terrorism currently practiced by the nuclear weapon states are criminal—not simply illegal, not simply immoral, but criminal under well-established principles of international law. This simple idea of the criminality of nuclear weapons can be utilized to pierce through the ideology of nuclearism to which many citizens in the nuclear weapons states have succumbed. It is with this simple idea of the criminality of nuclear weapons that such people can proceed to comprehend the inherent illegitimacy and fundamental lawlessness of the policies that their governments pursue in their names with respect to the further development of nuclear weapons systems.

The idea of the criminality of nuclear weapons is quite simple. And yet simple ideas are oftentimes the most powerful. For example, at one point in history, people saw no legal or moral problem with the institution of slavery. But as a result of the abolitionist movements in England and the United States, the entire international community eventually came around to the point of view that slavery and the slave trade were immoral, illegal, and criminal and therefore must be abolished and repressed, which they were and still are today. The same type of moral and perceptual transformation must occur now with respect to nuclear weapons among the citizenry in those states that possess them.

In all fairness, however, I should point out that there are today tens of thousands of people in the United States of America who truly believe that nuclear weapons are criminal under well-recognized principles of international law that have been fully subscribed to by the United States government and incorporated into United States domestic law. That number is increasing every day. Furthermore, there are hundreds of thousands of people in Europe, Canada, and the Western Pacific who believe that nuclear weapons systems are criminal, and that number is increasing every day. Finally, there are tens of millions of people around the world who believe that nuclear weapons systems are criminal. It therefore becomes necessary for all of us to further propagate the idea of the criminality of nuclear weapons in order to increase the number of people who hold that opinion in the United States as well as in the other nuclear weapons states for the purpose of compelling them to consider developing constructive strategies for the abolition of nuclear weapons from the face of the Earth.

THE CRIMINAL CONSPIRACY OF NUCLEAR DETERRENCE/TERRORISM

Humankind must abolish nuclear weapons before nuclear weapons abolish humankind. Nonetheless, a small number of governments in the world community continue to maintain nuclear weapons systems despite the rules of international criminal law to the contrary. This has led some international lawyers to argue, quite tautologically, that since there exist a few nuclear weapons states in the world community, nuclear weapons must somehow not be criminal because otherwise these few states would not possess nuclear weapons systems. In other words, to use lawyers' parlance, this minority-state practice of nuclear deterrence/terrorism by the great powers somehow negates the existence of a world *opinio juris* (i.e., sense of legal obligation) as to the criminality of nuclear weapons.

There is a very simple response to that specious argument: Since when has a small gang of criminals—in this case, the nuclear weapons states—been able to determine what is legal or illegal for the rest of the community by means of their own criminal behavior? What right do these nuclear weapons states have to argue that by means of their own criminal behavior they have *ipso facto* made criminal acts legitimate? No civilized nation state would permit a small gang of criminal conspirators to pervert its domestic legal order in this manner. Moreover, both the Nuremberg Tribunal and the Tokyo Tribunal made it quite clear that a conspiratorial band of criminal states likewise has no right to opt out of the international legal order by means of invoking their own criminal behavior as the least common denominator of international deportment.

THE HUMAN RIGHT TO ANTINUCLEAR CIVIL RESISTANCE

To the contrary, the entire human race has been victimized by an international conspiracy of ongoing criminal activity carried out by the nuclear weapons states under the doctrine known as "nuclear deterrence," which is really a euphemism for "nuclear terrorism." This international criminal conspiracy of nuclear deterrence/terrorism currently practiced by the nuclear weapons states is no different from any other conspiracy by a criminal gang or band. They are the outlaws. So it is up to the rest of the international community to repress and dissolve this international criminal conspiracy as soon as possible and by whatever nonviolent means are available.

In light of the fact that nuclear weapons systems are prohibited, illegal, and criminal under all circumstances and for any reason, every person around the world possesses a basic human right to be free from this criminal practice of nuclear deterrence/terrorism and its concomitant specter of nuclear extinction. Thus, all human beings possess the basic right under international law to engage in nonviolent civil resistance activities for the purpose of preventing, impeding, or terminating the ongoing commission of these international crimes. Every citizen of the world community has both the right and the duty to oppose the existence of nuclear weapons systems by whatever nonviolent means are at his or her disposal.

THE NUCLEAR PERVERSION OF CONSTITUTIONAL DEMOCRACY AND THE RULE OF LAW

In the United States, there are several ramifications that follow ineluctably from the conspiratorial doctrine and practice known as nuclear deterrence/terrorism. First, criminality is said to be legitimacy. When nuclear weapons were first developed and used, there was absolutely no consideration given to the rule of law. Thus, nuclear weapons represent the absolute negation of a rule of law both at home and abroad. The very existence of nuclear weapons requires that the rule of law be subverted both at home and abroad. Furthermore, nuclear weapons are antidemocratic. There has never been any form of meaningful democratic accountability applied to the U.S. nuclear weapons establishment. The American people as individuals or as a whole have never had any significant input into the process of developing nuclear weapons systems except to the extent that Congress has voted blank checks. The very existence of nuclear weapons systems and their requisite degrees of super-secrecy require that our system of nuclear government be kept stealthily antidemocratic.

Finally, the same principles hold true for the U.S. Constitution. Constitutional protections became meaningless when nuclear weapons were integrated into the U.S. foreign affairs and defense establishment. Indeed, the U.S. Constitution has become a farce and a facade in the name of national security as a direct result of nuclear weapons. In a similar manner, fundamental principles of legality, democracy, and constitutionality have been trampled under foot by all the nuclear weapons states in their mad stampede toward humankind's nuclear abyss.

Nuclear deterrence/terrorism as currently practiced by today's nuclear weapons states—this small gang of international criminal conspirators—cannot succeed over the long run because it is premised upon assumptions and practices that are immoral, illegal, unconstitutional, criminal, and irrational in the estimation of the respective public opinions in the various nuclear weapons states as well as around the world. Unless it is destroyed, nuclear deterrence/terrorism will ultimately fail and destroy all of humankind because of its own inherent contradictions. In particular, the assumptions, policies, and practices underlying the U.S. nuclear weapons establishment are irrational and insane from any meaningful perspective. Nevertheless, this conspiratorial doctrine of nuclear deterrence/terrorism has required that what is inherently irrational and insane somehow be made to appear to be completely rational and sane. America has quite necessarily had to invert and pervert its entire system of democratic values, legal ethos, and constitutional practices in order to account for and accommodate the existence of nuclear weapons.

THE IRRATIONALITY OF IRRATIONALITY

For example, a good deal of the U.S. nuclear weapons establishment and nuclear deterrence/terrorist practices are premised upon the Harvard political scientist Thomas Schelling's theory known as the "rationality of irrationality" that was expounded in his classic book *The Strategy of Conflict* (1960).

According to this pernicious doctrine, in theory it could sometimes prove to be a rational strategy for a government decision-maker to pretend to be completely irrational in his dealings with other states in order to get his own way. Adolph Hitler was said to be the paradigmatic example of this phenomenon during the 1930s. The outbreak of World War II in 1939, however, demonstrates the severe limitations of Schelling's theory with respect to nuclear weapons.

Applying Schelling's concept to nuclear weapons, an analyst could mistakenly come to the conclusion that it might prove to be useful for a government to threaten to commit the completely irrational and insane act of starting a nuclear war in order to avoid a conventional or nuclear war, or more cynically and realistically, to achieve certain geopolitical objectives. Furthermore, in order to make this insane threat credible, the threatening state must then supposedly proceed to develop the capability to launch and wage a nuclear war so that in the eyes of its intended adversary the completely irrational threat might begin to look somewhat more rational. When the adversary inevitably responds in kind, these psychological and bureaucratic dynamics produce the momentum needed for generating the self-fulfilling prophecy of nuclear Armageddon.

I will not bother here to analyze at any length the logical contradictions and psychological fallacies of U.S. nuclear deterrence/terrorism doctrine since that task has already been performed quite admirably by Robert Jervis in his definitive work on *The Illogic of American Nuclear Strategy* (1984). But I simply wish to point out that the entire theory of nuclear deterrence/terrorism as currently practiced by the world's nuclear weapons states represents a working out of Schelling's hypothesis propounding the "rationality of irrationality." All of the world's nuclear weapons states, and especially the two nuclear superpowers, have spent the past forty-five years trying to make a completely irrational threat appear to be rational and in the process have had to pervert and destroy all elements of rationality, legality, constitutionality, morality, and sanity that stood in their way. That task itself is ultimately doomed to failure unless and until the citizens of the world's nuclear weapons states can figure out some practical means to eliminate nuclear weapons before nuclear weapons eliminate them.

THE ILLEGAL STATUS OF NUCLEAR ARMS CONTROL AGREEMENTS

These observations then logically bring us to the question of the international legal status of nuclear arms control agreements. From the perspective developed above, nuclear arms control agreements are simply part of an international criminal conspiracy between a small gang of criminal states that are designed to further perpetuate the conspiracy. Nuclear arms control agreements attempt to rationalize, regularize, modernize, and perfect the instrumentalities of international criminal activity and mass extermination. Hence, they are entitled to no validity at all as a matter of positive international law.

Nevertheless, until humankind can get rid of those instrumentalities of crime, it is probably preferable to try to control nuclear weapons than not to try to control them. To be sure, a compelling argument can be made that nuclear arms control negotiations and agreements have never constituted more than soporifics designed by the nuclear weapons states, and especially by the two superpowers, to lull world public opinion into a false sense of trust in the process while, under their deceptive guise, these governments have pursued an unrelenting nuclear arms build-up and modernization. It appears that START I will be no exception to this general rule. Yet, whatever position one ultimately takes on this latter issue, we must never forget that all forms of nuclear arms control treaties concluded between the United States and the former Soviet Union and among the nuclear weapons states themselves still deal with these instrumentalities of internationally criminal and lawless behavior.

Thus, nuclear arms control agreements can only constitute a temporary expedient. Their overall objective must always remain that prescribed by article 6 of the 1968 Nuclear Non-Proliferation Treaty. To reiterate: "Each of the Parties to the Treaty undertakes to pursue negotiations in good faith on effective measures relating to cessation of the nuclear arms race at an early date and to nuclear disarmament, and on a treaty on general and complete disarmament under strict and effective international control." Universal nuclear disarmament is the only legally defensible, morally acceptable, and logically consistent position that can be taken.

THE STRATEGIC DEFENSE INITIATIVE

Unfortunately, the prospects for meaningful strategic nuclear arms reductions were seriously set back by the Reagan administration's proclamation of the so-called Strategic Defense Initiative (SDI) in 1983. That act represented nothing less than a formal statement by the United States government of its intention to pursue a policy that will eventually result in the commission of numerous material breaches of the 1972 U.S.-USSR Anti-Ballistic Missile Systems (ABM) Treaty. In other words, the SDI program actually constitutes an anticipatory repudiation of the ABM Treaty itself. In addition, SDI would probably violate the 1967 Outer Space Treaty, which prohibits the deployment of some of SDI's envisioned weapons of mass destruction in outer space. Moreover, field testing some of SDI's proposed technologies (e.g., the X-ray laser) would violate the path breaking 1963 Limited Test Ban Treaty, which specifically prohibits any type of nuclear explosion in outer space. Finally, the Reagan administration invoked the supposed need to test SDI technology as one of the grounds for its refusal to resume negotiations with the former Soviet Union over the conclusion of a Comprehensive Test Ban Treaty (CTBT).

We must call upon the United States government to reaffirm its commitment to the clear language as well as to its longstanding interpretation of the ABM Treaty and, therefore, to immediately terminate the SDI program. Furthermore, the ABM Treaty must be strengthened by the conclusion of a separate international convention that prohibits the development, testing, and deployment of antisatellite weapons systems, which can also be used for SDI purposes. Finally, the U.S. and the Russian Federation must clarify the limited scope of permissible "research" under the ABM Treaty by means of concluding a supplementary protocol for that purpose.

COMPREHENSIVE TEST BAN TREATY

The decision by the Reagan administration to reject the invitation by the former Soviet government to duplicate its imposition of a unilateral moratorium on the underground testing of nuclear weapons upon the occasion of the fortieth anniversary of the atomic bombing of Hiroshima was deplorable. Under the aforementioned principles of international law, all of the nuclear weapons states are obligated to impose an immediate moratorium on the design, testing, development, deployment, and modernization of all forms of nuclear weapons and their attendant delivery and communications systems. Those concerned nuclear weapons states must also return to the negotiations for the conclusion of a Comprehensive Test Ban Treaty, which were unilaterally suspended by the United States government in 1980. The successful conclusion of a CTBT under strict national and international verification would serve as a significant impediment to the faster acceleration of the nuclear arms race as well as to the further proliferation of nuclear weapons around the world.

NUCLEAR PROLIFERATION

To a significant extent, the proliferation of nuclear weapons and the capability to produce them can be directly attributable to the failure of the concerned nuclear weapons states, and especially the two superpowers, "to pursue negotiations in good faith on effective measures relating to cessation of the nuclear arms race at an early date and to nuclear disarmament . . . " as required by article 6 of the 1968 Nuclear Non-Proliferation Treaty. We must call upon the concerned nuclear weapons states to strictly discharge their solemn obligations under NPT Article 6. We must also urge those acknowledged nuclear weapons states that have not yet accepted the NPT to become parties. Finally, we must encourage those states that possess the capability to construct nuclear weapons but have not yet accepted the NPT to become parties and thereby expressly renounce any nuclear intentions. The security of states is fatally threatened, not protected, by the acquisition or development of a nuclear weapons capability. In addition to joining the NPT regime, the security of non-nuclear weapons states in various regions around the world can best be promoted by means of the mechanisms envisioned by Chapter VIII of the United Nations Charter on Regional Arrangements.

NUCLEAR-FREE ZONES

Significant progress by the two superpowers in the areas of reducing strategic nuclear weapons and preventing space weapons can facilitate the complete elimination of nuclear weapons systems at the regional level. In this regard, we must commend the efforts by governments, statesmen, and private individuals around the world to establish so-called "nuclear-free zones" in Europe, Latin America, and the South Pacific, etc. It would also be a positive development to establish nuclear-free zones at the national, state, and local levels as well. In this regard, I would like to suggest that the best way to start the life of the new united State of Germany would be for the German people to declare their new capital, Berlin, to be a nuclear-free zone. In addition, building upon existing treaties, the nuclear-free zone principle should be applied on a permanent and universal basis to outer space, Antarctica, the deep sea bed, the Arctic Ocean, the Indian Ocean, Africa, and the Middle East, *inter alia*. The progressive development of the nuclear-free zone movement has the potential to close off large sections of the global commons to the criminal activities by the nuclear weapons states and to the further proliferation of nuclear weapons.

THE RULE OF INTERNATIONAL LAW

We must reaffirm our unswerving commitment to the rule of international law, to the peaceful settlement of international disputes, to upholding the integrity of the United Nations Charter, and to respecting the authority of the International Court of Justice. Pursuant to this commitment, we must urge the membership of the U.N. General Assembly to give serious consideration to the conclusion of an international convention that expressly criminalizes the possession, design, testing, development, manufacture, deployment, use, and threat of use of "nuclear weapons" specifically by that name. Moreover, the General Assembly must give urgent consideration to further steps that would lead to the complete elimination of nuclear weapons from the face of the Earth. In particular, the General Assembly should request an Advisory Opinion from the International Court of Justice on the general subject of Nuclear Weapons and International Law. *A sound repudiation of the alleged legality of the threat or use of nuclear weapons and of the nuclear arms race by the International Court of Justice would go a long way toward convincing the entire international community that nuclear weapons are not legitimate instruments of state policy, but rather manifestations of lawlessness and criminality.*

CONCLUSION

Admittedly, the agenda set forth above is ambitious, but under the specter of nuclear extinction, we have no alternative but to struggle for its achievement. We must call upon all jurists and human rights activists around the world, as well as all men and women of good faith everywhere, to join us in this crusade for universal nuclear disarmament. Otherwise, the human race will suffer the same fate as the dinosaurs, and the planet Earth will become a radioactive wasteland. The time for preventive action is now!

12 | MANOUTCHEHR M. ESKANDARI-QAJAR
The United Nations: Where Should We Go from Here?

The following essay is intended as a call for bold thought and action regarding that most amazing and idealistic of experiments: the United Nations. This is not a complete set of original prescriptions; there are many examples—some in the present volume—of more eloquent and more persuasive accounts of the need for a restructured United Nations along economic, legal, administrative, and other lines. The point here was neither to duplicate those accounts nor to outdo them. This essay is simply an attempt to revive a discussion that is as old as the first effort at international institution-building, the League of Nations. Learning from the failures of the League of Nations and the disappointments of a deadlocked United Nations, there is here an invitation to rethink the workings of this most promising of institutions with the hindsight of forty-seven years. What this essay suggests is that the nation-state and all its appendages are the stumbling blocks to change and that it is time to go beyond them.

There is an urgent question before us today that will require serious consideration: Should the United Nations be strengthened now to finally enable it to carry out all the functions the founding nations envisaged for it?

The new Secretary-General of the United Nations, Mr. Boutros-Ghali, has brought to his post a zeal and enthusiasm in the direction of strength and effectiveness that seem to indicate that change is coming soon. It remains to be seen, however, how much of his ambitious reorganization plan he will be able to put in place before old territorial forces and state pressures come to bear to derail this much-needed effort.

The question of a renewed and strengthened United Nations has two distinct elements. The first is the matter of whether or not this strengthening should take place at all. If it should, the second element is the question of how to achieve it. While the first is a political question, the second is a procedural one. Let us look at the political question first.

The United Nations is an organization of nation-states, or countries, as its name indicates. Fifty-one independent countries, five of which were winners of the second World War, created the organization as a successor to the ill-fated League of Nations. The chief defect of the League of Nations was the absence of the United States in its membership as the balancing element in the post-World War I power game. Painfully aware of the costs of this absence, there were among the founding fathers of the United Nations those who hoped that the United Nations would become a supranational organization that would supersede the nation-state and impose its will on the globe as the sole bearer and enforcer of international law. But there was also a sizable faction, notably among those who formed the Security Council, who were not at all thinking of giving up state sovereignty—the ultimate power of decision-making that nation-states abrogate to themselves— and in so doing they created the world of 1945 and, more or less, that of the next forty or so years. But since 1989 world events have changed dramatically, making the notion of inviolable state sovereignty and nation-state control of international organizations debatable again.

Most impressive among the recent international changes is, of course, the break-up of the Soviet sphere of influence in Eastern Europe and the subsequent disappearance of the Soviet Union itself. The dissolution of the Soviet Union has also opened up the possibility for the birth of several new states—both on former Soviet territory and in Eastern Europe. Some of these potential new states have nuclear and conventional arms far beyond their legitimate needs, which could thus result in the creation of many areas of concern where there was formerly just one.

Second in importance among the events accompanying the advent of this *novus ordo*, and not much noticed by the media until the recent conflict with Iraq, has been the rapid proliferation of nuclear weapons and other weapons of mass destruction in non-signatory states of the Non-Proliferation Treaty of 1968, especially among developing countries and nonpermanent members of the Security Council. Thus, while witnessing the simultaneous birth of an order we hesitatingly call the long-awaited "New World Order," we also find ourselves watching a world sink into potential chaos and intense international rivalry over the acquisition of nuclear and chemical capability and the struggle for statehood and "independence."

This combination of factors has created a watershed in international relations equaled only by the events leading to the founding of the United Nations itself. The founding of the United Nations, though not resulting in the abolition of state-sovereignty in general, strongly proclaimed the intolerability of certain kinds of applications of that sovereignty: war-making at the scale at which the Axis Powers envisaged it and non-adherence to internationally accepted norms of civilized behavior, to name two.

Today's fierce reassertion of national sovereignty and its attending quest for speedy armament and war-fighting capability, combined with the willingness to use any amount of lethal power acquired to achieve quick results, has indeed put us back in time to a situation similar to that which made the United Nations a necessary experiment for the sake of global survival. Though the logic for the call to arms has not changed, the alibis have, and this renewed quest for the ultimate means of destruction has to do with the recognition that nuclear power has been the determining factor in international relations since 1945. All these years, it appeared that those who had nuclear weapons could speak with authority, and those who did not were forced to listen. For many non-nuclear countries, this did not become an issue. They formed alliances, set their courses along different lines than those of military power, and prospered in the gulf between this battle of the titans. For other countries, however, whose thinking remained along traditional power terms, the race was on to get to the nuclear, chemical, or biological threshold. Some did so for fear of being left without protection should the superpowers withdraw theirs, others for fear of not being able to stake out and back up their political, territorial, or ideological claims, others still for the sheer opportunity to speak at par with the "Big Five," realizing that might, if not making right, at least gave one the power to have one's voice heard and one's concerns taken seriously.

For almost five decades, the fact that super nation-states could decide the fate of the globe held the world both hostage and oddly in abeyance. That the limits of the nation-state were not questioned then had to do with the power of those who would have to do such questioning and the rivalry among them. Today, however, that rivalry is over, and with it the world that sustained such a stalemate. The very powers who were opposed to discussion on such crucial matters as world peace and disarmament are sitting side by side at the conference tables to condemn the proliferation of arms and abuses of human rights in recognition of the impending disaster that is the legacy of their old rivalry. Thus, the world is ready for a renewed discussion of the political question raised: Has the nation-state become obsolete as the final judge over the well-being of the globe? If that question is answered in the affirmative, then the question of strong, independent, but accountable, supranational organizations must again be raised, as should the question of neutral, central, international control of weapons of mass destruction.

The crucial issue of the survival of the human race can no longer be left to individual countries with their own short- and medium-range designs for self-defined "maximum" or even "minimum" security. The world must look to strengthened democratic international bodies, such as a renewed United Nations, to take over these paramount tasks.

The political question of a strengthened and renewed United Nations is, thus, no longer a question of what is politically correct, feasible, or achievable, while paying homage to ossified power structures. The politics of the question disappear more and more with the realization that the realities of the world at the end of the twentieth century are such that no one state, not even any one combination of states, can have all the answers to the problems the world is facing today. This recognition leads us to the inevitable conclusion that strong supranational bodies with global coordination and problem-solving capacities and guarantees of accountability are the only possible way out of the dilemmas we face and will increasingly face in the future.

If the answer to the first question is a resounding yes, out of necessity this brings us to the next aspect of the original question, the procedural element of it: How do we go about reaching the goal of a strengthened, democratically run United Nations?

The following proposals, even though ambitious in tone, and unthinkable three years ago, are, however, indispensable steps in the direction of that strengthened United Nations:

1. **CHARTER REVISION.** Charter-revision talks, in the form of a General Conference by the members of the General Assembly, as mandated by Article 109 of the United Nations Charter, but abandoned since the late fifties, should be given highest priority and revived immediately for the express purpose of creating the legal framework for the crucial changes proposed below. These changes will provide both the constitutional foundation, as well as the moral impetus, for the kind of organization the United Nations needs to be in order to fulfill its role in this world of new international realities.

2. **PERMANENT MEMBERSHIP IN THE SECURITY COUNCIL.** The notion of permanent membership in the Security Council was linked to the end of World War II, the avoidance of a recurrence of such a disaster, and the newfound strength-in-unity of its founding members. It was also based on a notion of power that a few years later would reflect itself in the nuclear capability of the "Big Five." Another aspect of the founding philosophy was the notion that "enemy states," Japan and Germany specifically, were to be kept out of the running of the organization to avoid a replay of the just-finished war.

All of these notions have now become obsolete. Nuclear power, a precarious peacekeeper for the last four decades, has become a psychological burden on mankind. From a balance of power that kept the warring factions at bay, nuclear weapons created a balance of terror that held the world hostage. Japan and newly united Germany are no longer threats to world peace, rather they are upholders of international standards of cooperation and progress along democratic lines. They have also become economic superpowers demanding the recognition and respect countries of their standing deserve; in this case they demand permanent access to the Security Council. And then there is the majority of mankind represented by the amorphous concept of the "third" or "developing" world, with all that these terms subtly imply. What about them? Should they also have a place at this banquet of power? Will they wait for the West to resolve that question for itself and them?

An answer is readily available, and the climate seems ripe for it today. Two principles have held the Security Council hostage for all these years, and both have to do with the extension of the notion of national sovereignty into the international body: permanent membership on the council and the veto power of the "Big Five." Both of these principles are impediments, and both need to be replaced. Instead of the council consisting of five permanent members with veto power and ten rotating members, as it does now, there should be one council with fifteen members, who serve for a period of five or more years. Voting on all questions of military intervention or of similar gravity should be subject to an extraordinary majority, say two-thirds or even three-fourths. Voting on all other matters should be subject to a simple majority, with each member getting one vote. Finally, membership on the new Security Council should be rotational with the concurrence of the General Assembly—the only representative body in the United Nations from its inception—in accordance with a pre-agreed formula based on any one of the many existing decision-making practices now in use at the United Nations, taking into consideration economic, social, political, strategic, and other criteria for maximum fairness.

3. **PERMANENT INTERNATIONAL PEACEKEEPING FORCE.** One of the perennial weaknesses of the United Nations, and more generally of international law, has been the absence of United Nations enforcement power. This has led some to even question the very existence of international law and, thus, the legitimacy of any spokesperson for it. To go along with this wider distribution of power in its executive body and to avoid the frustration of having to sit idly by when the very foundational principles of international order are being undermined, the United Nations must have access to a permanent force under its direction that is independent of the political whims of its member states.

The financing of such a force can be arranged on the basis of quotas, with international lawbreakers bearing an additional punitive surcharge, for instance. The present Military Staff Committee of the council could function as its "Joint Chiefs" reporting to the Secretary-General and the council.

4. **NUCLEAR MONOPOLY UNDER UNITED NATIONS AUSPICES.** To give the United Nations' efforts teeth, all nuclear weapons should finally be placed under its supervision with military representatives of the present nuclear powers serving as trustees of these weapons under the aegis of the revamped Security Council. To these weapons could be added all other weapons of mass destruction. A regime of international verification and on-site inspection, free of the stumbling blocks of "domestic" spheres of influences and "internal affairs" that states can currently erect through the help of Article 2, section 7 of the Charter to shield themselves from independent observation, would also need to be created, as would a regime of global disarmament spearheaded by the United Nations' Global Disarmament Conference and enforced by its peacekeeping strength.

5. **INTERNATIONAL CHARTER OF HUMAN RIGHTS.** First, the terms "human rights" and "world citizenship" will have to be reiterated to include specifically men, women, and children, to eliminate the need for separate charters of rights and decades of reminders about each of these categories as if they were separate entities. Then, redundant as it may seem, a new international regime for the universal protection of human rights, as redefined by the United Nations General Assembly, must be put in place. This would mean, as mentioned above, that states would no longer have the right to hide behind national sovereignty in order to continue their business-as-usual treatment of peoples placed arbitrarily under their supreme and unquestionable power and whim by the vagaries of history and the ironies of situation-room mapmaking!

The United Nations must reaffirm, as the new "World Body" it will have become, that it has just as intrinsic a stake in the well-being of the citizens of the world as the individual states have had so far according to their domestic proclamations. If there is to be a saner world for us to live in, this principle must be upheld unequivocally by investing it with the full moral and political weight of the United Nations. Once established in principle that the United Nations is, in fact, the guardian of the well-being of the citizens of the world, then discussions can commence on the expansion of this notion of well-being, based perhaps on such precedents as President Roosevelt's "Four Freedoms," which not only speak of freedom from fear and persecution, but also include prominently the notion of economic rights (freedom from want), without which the talk of human rights will always remain an empty proclamation.

6. **WORLD CITIZENSHIP.** Finally, and perhaps most symbolically, the United Nations could work toward the achievement of this notion of a new international charter of human rights by actively lobbying for the acceptance of a new World Citizen Passport and Citizenship Document, which would replace the present passport and citizenship requirements imposed by individual countries. The adoption of such a universally valid document would further erode the notion that by virtue of citizenship or residence in a particular country, governments can limit the freedom of individuals. It would also severely curtail the abuse of human rights currently suffered by many because of their dependence on their governments for internationally valid identification and, thus, internationally recognizable identity. A world passport and citizenship document backed by the full moral and political force of a newly reconstituted United Nations would give the United Nations the legal as well as the moral right to speak for these voiceless, and now often hopeless, citizens of the world.

As in 1945, we are now once again at a threshold. We have to decide if we want to keep the world order as we find it, or change it so that the world that would emerge as the result of our efforts would be a safer, sounder, and healthier one. The task of building such a world requires the courage and determination to make the necessary changes in those institutions that can make a difference. The United Nations is one such institution, and as much hope rests on it today as did at its founding, when the words "to rid the world of the scourge of war" were spoken with full conviction and commensurate boldness and hope.

13 | JAN TINBERGEN
A More Effective
United Nations

Great problems in today's world can no longer be solved by decisions of sovereign national states. Interconnections among nations have grown to such an extent that such decisions inevitably
affect the welfare of other nations. Economists call this process "external effects." Too often national decision-making processes fail to
consider the welfare of other countries.

This study discusses the four great problems presently facing the
world and suggests that the United Nations is the system which, after a
revitalization, may best meet the world's needs for decision-making at
a global level.

THE FOUR GREAT PROBLEMS

Today the world is faced with four great problems the solutions to
which are vital to the future of humankind:

1. **SECURITY POLICY**: the problem of preventing war, in particular,
nuclear war;

2. **ENVIRONMENT POLICY**: the problem of improving and maintaining the quality of the environment in which life, particularly human
life, develops;

3. **THIRD WORLD DEVELOPMENT POLICY**: the problem of providing
adequate economic assistance to underdeveloped countries;

4. **SUSTAINABILITY POLICY**: the problem of protecting natural resources for the use of future generations.

This chapter will treat each of these four problems in turn and
conclude with recommendations for creating a more effective United
Nations.

SECURITY POLICY

Throughout history, most politicians have accepted war as a permissible means of settling conflicts. In Hannes Alfvén's words, only when weapons became "annihilators" did a majority of people become aware of the senselessness of war. Nuclear annihilators introduced the risk that all human beings would be killed, including those who had started the war. The only benefit of nuclear weapons has been that the hawks have joined the doves, and that global security has become a widely accepted aim of international policy.

Avoiding nuclear war is the precondition for all other human activities. After a long period of Cold War mentality, the superpowers are engaged in the process of disarmament, as recommended by a variety of scientists and other experts.

Disarmament is, of course, essential to any plan for increasing global security. Considered in isolation, disarmament means a reduction of employment. Greater emphasis must be placed on producing goods and services needed to solve the world's four great problems. This redirection of production is called conversion, and a policy of disarmament will be accelerated if conversion is increased. The experience of World War II shows that, during the period immediately following the war, conversion operated smoothly.

In discussing issues of global security, it is useful to apply the theory of the optimum level of decision-making. This theory states that the best level of decision-making is the lowest level at which all individuals affected by a given decision are represented. If, for example, a decision must be made that only affects the welfare of the local population, the optimum level of decision-making is at the local level.

It is my belief that decisions that affect the welfare of only one republic of the Commonwealth of Independent States can and should be made by that republic. Decisions that affect the welfare of other republics should be made at the lowest level 'where these republics share representation. Similarly, Eastern Europe's problem is that its welfare has been harmed by an imposed social order. Security assistance as an instrument of peace policy is being discussed as a means of compensating for the damage inflicted by the Yalta conference. [1] The basis for deciding the amount and type of this assistance must be determined; however, it represents an opportunity for the superpowers to make an important contribution toward global security.

Today many countries, especially large ones, do not accept "interference with internal affairs," because they consider themselves "sovereign" nations. A necessary and crucial step in the creation of a peaceful world is that part of each nation's sovereignty be surrendered to a higher level of government. In principle, such transfers of national sovereignty are needed for the welfare of other nations to be taken into account.

Up to now, responsibility for the United Nations peacemaking process has been the task of the Security Council, the Secretary-General, the International Court of Justice, and several United Nations interim forces, such as the U.N. force in Cyprus or the U.N. interim force in Lebanon. These operations require reform to improve their effectiveness.

For example, the Security Council could operate more effectively if its permanent members, those with nuclear arms (United States, Commonwealth of Independent States, China, France, United Kingdom) had no veto power. The contribution to peacekeeping made by the International Court of Justice would be more effective if sanctions were imposed on nations refusing to abide by judgments of the court. This plan would also increase respect for the decisions of the court.

To achieve global security, it is also necessary for U.N. forces to become a permanent rather than *ad hoc* institution, comparable to various forms of police in every well-organized community. Thus a new agency, to be called the United Nations Police Force, could be substituted for the *ad hoc* forces created in the past.

In 1967, the "Treaty on Principles Governing the Activities of States in the Exploration and Use of Outer Space, Including the Moon and Other Celestial Bodies" promoted international cooperation in the exploration and use of outer space. There is potential for the creation of a U.N. agency that will support a new Law of Outer Space to define and maintain the peaceful uses of space. Ratification of the Law of the Sea will play an equally important role in maintaining global security.

ENVIRONMENTAL POLICY

Pollution in its various forms has considerably diminished the quality of our surroundings. Manufacturing, traffic, and agriculture have introduced many toxic materials and gases, which are killing our forests and polluting our rivers and the atmosphere. Biologists continuously report on the extinction of entire species of animals and plants. Accidents with nuclear energy plants (Chernobyl, Three Mile Island), oil tankers (Alaska, Morocco), and pharmaceutical factories (Bhopal, India; Basle, Switzerland) threaten human life; smog covers cities all over the globe.

An increasing number of people understand the need for an active policy against further pollution. The importance of environmental policies was demonstrated by the extraordinary interest in the biannual meeting of the United Nations Environment Programme (UNEP) in 1989 at which 103 delegates, including forty-four government ministers, were present. Donor countries committed themselves to raise the budget from $30 million to $100 million in two years. Binding legislation to protect biological diversity was recommended, and a world climate fund was established.

Experts on environmental problems and solutions emphasize the need for quick action. If necessary measures are delayed, the damage being done will accelerate and the costs of the cure will rise disproportionally. Here, a fundamental difficulty arises. The reforms of our decision-making structure show an inverse tendency: they become easier if more time is available for their execution. In principle, the best policy is the one in which total costs are held to a minimum. The estimation of the costs thus becomes an important instrument of policy and needs research.

Some environmental measures can be decided by national or even local authorities, such as maintaining satisfactory levels of soil quality. However, other measures must be taken at a supranational and even global level. Keeping an important river clean may be a task for the group of countries through which that river flows. Pollution of the oceans and of the atmosphere can be reduced only by measures at the global level. UNEP is the appropriate agency to design these measures. There must also be instruments to enforce the execution of environmental measures. UNEP must be given the task of supervising member countries and of applying sanctions if environmental policies of a country do not meet UNEP criteria.

Technological development has also affected the seas and oceans. Although oceans cover three-fourths of the Earth's surface, they can no longer be considered large enough to absorb the waste products of industry. At the same time, manganese nodules on the ocean floor may constitute a new source of profitable production. These factors make management of the oceans a necessity and require that the existing Law of the Sea be replaced.

In 1967 Ambassador Arvid Pardo of Malta addressed the U.N. General Assembly, stressing the peaceful use of the oceans and also the use of their natural resources to benefit all humankind. Pardo argued that the ocean's resources outside the Exclusive Economic Zones (EEZs) around the coastal nations had not so far been claimed by any nation and that these riches could be used to aid underdeveloped nations.

In 1968 a Seabed Committee was appointed, and in 1971 a treaty banning nuclear and other weapons of mass destruction from the ocean seabeds was signed. In 1975 the U.N. Conference on the Law of the Sea was established and, after nine years of negotiations, the text of the law was formulated. The law states that ocean management would be organized by joint ventures of an official international enterprise, with private Western enterprises supplying the technology.

Unfortunately, a group of Western firms interested in mining the manganese nodules are attempting to keep their technologies to themselves, thus depriving poor countries of the revenue Pardo intended to be shared by the world community. The Law of the Sea has yet to be ratified.

There is much similarity between the oceans and outer space. Both are universal elements, existing outside national boundaries. As a result of scientific and technological progress, both can yield useful services to the world economy. These similarities constitute a good argument for the establishment of a Law of Outer Space and a U.N. Space Agency. Though the Outer Space Treaty was concluded in

1967, what we need is an institution with the authority to impose an optimum policy, i.e., one that maximizes world welfare.

A positive feature in both the Outer Space Treaty and the Law of the Sea is their adherence to the principle of "common heritage." This principle, proposed by former Ambassador Pardo, is that the oceans and outer space form a "common heritage" that should be used in the interests of the world as a whole and, more particularly, the underdeveloped countries.

THIRD WORLD DEVELOPMENT POLICY

All industrialized nations have a government agency that makes available developmental assistance to developing countries—either directly or indirectly—through U.N. agencies. The most important United Nations agencies are the World Bank Group and the International Monetary Fund. Other agencies include the Food and Agricultural Organization (FAO), International Fund for Agricultural Development (IFAD), United Nations Industrial Development Organization (UNIDO), United Nations Development Program (UNDP), United Nations International Children's Emergency Fund (UNICEF), and World Health Organization (WHO).

Development cooperation is looked upon skeptically because of doubts about the efficiency of U.N. agencies and because of the existence of fraud. Partly as a consequence of these problems, the amounts made available are, on average, only 0.35 percent of Gross National Product (GNP). This is half the norm of 0.7 percent recommended by the Pearson Committee in 1969 and the Brandt Commission in 1980 and 1983.

The basis for calculating the 0.7 percent figure is not very clear. Recently I estimated the time needed to equalize incomes of developed and underdeveloped countries. With the present old level (0.35 per cent of GNP) five hundred years are needed.[2] With 0.7 percent of GNP that time would be reduced to 493 years only. In order to attain equalized incomes in 460 years, 3 percent of GNP would be needed. So, a level of official development assistance of 2 percent of the GNP would be a very modest step.

As most donor countries have contributed less than half of 0.7 percent to date, institutions that represent the world community—such as the World Bank and International Monetary Fund—could be reformed and strengthened to play an important role by being authorized to determine the contribution of each donor country.

In addition, since international trade is the other source from which underdeveloped countries can finance their development, a reform in the field of international trade seems natural. Reforming and strengthening UNCTAD (United Nations Conference on Trade and Development) and GATT (General Agreement on Trade and Tariffs) may be helpful, as well as the establishment of an International Trade Organization (ITO) with the power to prohibit some forms of international trade policy.

The necessity of more equitable income distribution between developed and underdeveloped countries is understood, but the need is not being met. Data on the development of world income inequality have been published by Summers[3] and by Theil.[4] The most important message from both sources is that international income inequality has changed only slightly since 1950.

Many reports evaluating the present forms of development assistance are available. They testify that the quality of that assistance can be improved. Many forms of waste are reported, such as machines arriving before a factory is built or unnecessary losses of food occurring during transportation. Corruption is also common at many levels of government.

More development aid is not only necessary for the receiving countries, but it is also in the best interests of donor countries. Since no improvement in world income distribution has occurred, prosperous countries are flooded by immigrants from underdeveloped countries. North America is inundated with people from Latin America; Western Europe by Arab and Turkish immigrants; and the rich oil countries by citizens of surrounding Arab nations and Pakistan. Legal and illegal immigrants compete in the labor and housing markets, and, especially in Europe, different cultural backgrounds create conflicts that contribute to fear and hatred.

The plight of underdeveloped countries can hardly be discussed today unless the problem of their large debts to foreign governments is addressed. The magnitude of the total external debt is $1 trillion. For all underdeveloped countries, GNP is less than $3 trillion. It seems relevant to compare this figure with the amount of "development assistance backlog," meaning the assistance that would have been available if all donor countries had given 0.7 percent of their GNP. This backlog is almost $0.5 trillion. In other words, the current external debt would have been half as large if the donor countries had held to the norm of 0.7 percent. If the 2 percent norm had been applied, presumably no debt problem would exist.

A clear summary of how the debt problem came about is offered by Professor H. W. Singer.[5] He points out that for quite some time, borrowing by foreign governments and banks was welcomed by the World Bank and the International Monetary Fund as a complement to their lending. Recently, when it appeared that the anticipated effects of such borrowing were not obtained, the debt situation became a debt tragedy and a subject of concern in the World Council of Churches and other nongovernmental organizations. The well-known Mexican economist Victor Urquidi made the imaginative proposal that part of the interest payments could be paid, in local currency, into an account that would finance investment projects approved by the creditor country. This system was applied in the Marshall Plan in Europe after World War II.[6]

It seems reasonable to conclude that lending governments should take responsibility for a large part of the debt burden in underdeveloped countries.

SUSTAINABILITY POLICY

Nearly every human being feels responsible for his or her children and, in turn, for their children's children. Thinking of the future macroeconomically, society feels responsible for future generations. This responsibility results in concern for conservation of the environment and its resources, such as energy, metal ores, and agricultural potential.

The necessity of sustainability, pointed out by the Brundtland Report, *Our Common Future,*[7] is understood by the experts, but has had little effect on today's policies. Sustainability means that the current generation should use a limited portion of exhaustible natural resources, ensuring their availability to future generations.

Knowing that the quantity of natural resources is finite, is it possible to use such resources for an infinite number of future generations? In order to understand the nature of this problem, we will reduce it to its simplest form. We will assume that:

1. Population is stationary.
2. The volume of goods and services consumed by the population is constant over time.
3. Technological progress exists and reduces the quantity p of natural resources available to produce a unit of consumer goods and services each year by a factor p (for example, 0.98).

Let the consumption and investment of goods and services in each year be r. Through some simple high school algebra, we can show that the quantity of natural resources needed to produce goods and services for all future generations is finite indeed, namely $r/(1 - p)$, or 50 r, if $p = 0.98$. Of these total resources, we must not use more than r, in our example 1/50 of the resources available. If p were increased, the quantity of resources needed would increase, and the amount that we would be permitted to use without damaging the interests of future generations would decrease. For energy, where $p = 0.9835$, we must not use more than about 1/60 of the known reserves.

Our simplified example ignores the fact that population is not remaining constant, but is rising. Also, technological progress may not be as strong as assumed. Can technological development go on forever? Some optimism about continuing innovation by the human race seems legitimate.

In all cases, an effective population policy will be one of the conditions for a solution to the population/resources problem. The population of developed countries is expected to stabilize around the year 2030. Stability in the populations of underdeveloped countries is not predicted to occur by that date.

Technological progress will also be an important solution to problems of sustainability. The encouragement of scientific research, combined with the protection of a patent system and prizes for technological innovation, will help stimulate technological development. When addressing problems of sustainability, it should be noted that delays make the solutions much more costly, and that the amount of energy reserves needed also increases rapidly the longer we postpone action. The costs after one year's delay are moderate. After two years, they are about three times as large; after three years, costs are six times as large; after four years, almost ten times as large; and after five years, fourteen times as large. Such an acceleration of costs serves as a good indication of the problem's urgency.

LEVELS OF SUPRANATIONAL DECISION-MAKING

The phrase "supranational" covers a variety of higher-than-national decision levels. Decisions based on treaties concluded by a limited number of countries are good examples. Benelux is an example of three cooperating nations: Belgium, the Netherlands, and Luxembourg. Decisions about the quality of Rhine water constitute an example of cooperation between five countries. Decisions of the European Community may bind twelve nations. If, in the future, the Economic Commissions for Europe (ECE), for Latin America (ECLAC), for Africa (ECA), and the Economic and Social Commission for Asia and the Pacific (ESCAP) can make binding decisions, then supranational decision-making will apply to continents.

The highest level of decision-making is the global level. Security, the environmental quality of oceans and the atmosphere, assistance to underdeveloped countries, sustainable development, and problems of health and population are examples of areas in which global decisions are needed.

Managed optimally, our planet will require a number of institutions authorized to make policies for all nations. At present, most of the necessary institutions do not exist. Examples do exist, however, of similar institutions operating in a more limited sphere. A well-known example in Western Europe is the High Authority for Coal and Steel, initiated by Jean Monnet. The distinctive feature of that authority is its transnational nature: without involving national governments, the authority decides on investments in coal mining, steel production, and other items by individual enterprises.

NEW UNITED NATIONS AGENCIES PROPOSED

1. A WORLD TREASURY. The membership contribution paid by each member nation to the United Nations proper (excluding specialized agencies) is fixed by the General Assembly. For the years 1989 to 1991, the amounts are recorded in the Report of the Committee on Contributions.[8] These amounts are based on the "capacity to pay" (population multiplied by the income per capita). Some limits are applied: no member must pay less than .01 percent or more than 25 percent of the expenditures to be financed. In addition, a further limitation is set forth in the report to avoid excessive variations in assessment rates between successive scales. Contributions to specialized agencies are determined in a similar way.

At present, each United Nations agency takes care of funding its own activities. A list of such activities given by the U.S. State Department in the 33rd Annual Report on U.S. Contributions to International Organizations contains over one hundred items, including approximately fifty United Nations special programs and specialized agencies.[9] Funding is carried out inefficiently, with an enormous duplication of work and lack of cooperation. One single World Treasury would eliminate this duplication.

The World Treasury would define the amount of bilateral development assistance required of each member nation, in addition to defining the amounts each nation should contribute to the United Nations and its specialized agencies. Each member country would pay the total of a specified list of contributions, and the World Treasury would also supervise collection of these monies. One World Treasury would be able to coordinate the total revenues received by each specialized agency or by each activity of the U.N.

It would be preferable to leave the funding of the World Bank Group and the International Monetary Fund in the hands of those agencies, just as in well-governed nations the Investment Bank and the Central Bank are independent institutions. This comparison with well-governed countries also illustrates the importance of a World Treasury; inside each country the Treasury (or Ministry of Finance) is the core of the government.

2. **A WORLD POLICE FORCE.** In the world community, law and order must be maintained. Special agencies exist within the U.N. to address this task of primary importance, for example, the Security Council. A general and permanent institution designated as the World Police Force must also be created. Its responsibility would be to identify and correct illegal behavior by any agency or member country. Each case discovered might be brought before the International Court of Justice. If the court's ruling are disregarded, sanctions would then be imposed. These sanctions might be economic, such as fines or cessation of commercial trade. In cases of persistent illegal behavior, the World Police Force would have the means to deploy military force.

The United Nations has some experience in the use of force—for instance, in the Congo, Cyprus, and Lebanon. These forces were created *ad hoc*, for a limited period of time only. The World Police Force would be a permanent institution, composed of regularly changing troops and administrative personnel.

3. **A SPACE AGENCY.** The use of outer space must be based on a Law of Outer Space, for which proposals have already been made. A conference similar to the United Nations Conference on the Law of the Sea should be convened to discuss and draft a Law of Outer Space.

Among the peaceful uses of outer space, the launching of various types of satellites is important. Better knowledge of the Earth and its riches can be obtained by remote sensing, including observation and photography from satellites. Satellites may also be used for weather forecasts, communication of television programs, and observation of treaties implemented by United Nations institutions.

Some spacecraft may have destinations other than satellites. Nearer destinations would be shuttle services to other countries or continents. Further destinations would be the moon or other planets in our solar system.

At present, the Outer Space Division, which serves the Committee on Peaceful Uses of Outer Space and its two subcommittees, coordinates and cooperates primarily with ITU (International Telecommunications Union), but also with WMO (World Meteorological Organization), INMARSAT (International Maritime Satellite Organization), and FAO (Food and Agriculture Organization). The new Space

Agency established by the Law of Outer Space would cooperate with these and other institutions.

THE BRANDT, PALME, AND BRUNDTLAND COMMISSIONS

Three important international commissions have dealt with the four great problems facing humankind in the last two decades. The members of these commissions were independent experts from all over the globe. The commissions were chaired by Willy Brandt, former Chancellor of the Federal Republic of Germany; Olof Palme, former Prime Minister of Sweden; and Dr. Gro Harlem Brundtland, Prime Minister of Norway.

The Brandt Commission dealt with international development issues; the Palme Commission with disarmament and security issues; and the Brundtland Commission with environment and development. Since the Brundtland Commission's findings included discussion of the responsibility for future generations, the reports of the commissions covered the four great problems discussed here.

The Brandt Report, *North-South: A Program for Survival*, states that "a globally respected peace-keeping mechanism should be built up—strengthening the role of the United Nations." The report concludes its recommendation on energy scarcity with the proposal that "a global energy research center should be created under U.N. auspices." It also states that "the reform of the international monetary system should be urgently undertaken."[10]

The Palme Report, *Common Security—A Blueprint for Survival*, recommends a more effective use of the Security Council and the Secretary-General of the U.N. The report discusses "an operational structure for U.N. standby forces," followed by four recommendations on strengthening the peacekeeping capacity of the United Nations and its members.[11]

The Brundtland Report, *Our Common Future*, advocates strengthening the United Nations Environmental Programme (UNEP). An urgent need for increased financial means is expressed, along with a "much higher sensitivity to environmental concerns." The imposition of taxes for polluting activities is suggested; the commission agrees with the Brandt Commission's proposals in this field. In conclusion, the Brundtland Report calls for the U.N. General Assembly to "transform this report into a U.N. Programme of Action on Sustainable Development."[12]

The parallels between the recommendations of these important reports and the ideas proposed in this chapter lead us to a review of the timetable for establishing a supranational decision-making system.

CHOICE OF A REFORMED UNITED NATIONS SYSTEM

The United Nations seems the best choice of a supranational decision-making body for an integrated world community. The U.N.'s advantages include the willingness of the superpowers to use its existing "family of institutions," its more than forty years of experience, and its complete representation of the world's nations.

However, at present, U.N. resolutions are not the decisions needed for an efficient world community. Strengthening the U.N. means changing its resolutions into binding decisions. The reformed and strengthened institutions charged with global management to solve the four great problems will be: the Security Council, the International Court of Justice, the United Nations Environmental Programme (or Agency), the World Bank, and the International Monetary Fund. In addition, numerous reformed specialized agencies, a reborn International Trade Organization, and three new agencies—a Space Agency, a World Treasury, and a World Police Force—will be needed.

The most important characteristic of this new world management is that it will be organized functionally, not geographically. As Van Benthem van den Bergh puts it, it will not be a (world) state, but a group of functional authorities.[13]

New information and research will be needed to help solve relatively new problems. The large deviation from conventional wisdom concerning development assistance proposed here—from 0.35 percent of GNP to 2 percent, a sixfold increase—will require well-founded research in order to have any chance of acceptance. Research is also needed on energy policy, population policy, and a policy of technological progress.

In order to carry out U.N. reforms, a series of meetings of the institutions and individuals involved will be needed. Timetables for the steps to be taken, and cost estimates for shorter and longer durations of the reform process must be made. In this way, a first impression will be obtained about the optimum timetable for various decisions.

THE GENERAL ASSEMBLY: VOTING RIGHTS

With the possible exception of the World Bank Group and the International Monetary Fund, the reformed and strengthened agencies will operate under the supervision of the U.N. General Assembly (the World Parliament). We must make a clear distinction between the power given to member nations and the technical aspects of implementing a desired power distribution. One study defined three methods of power distribution: 1) the dollar procedure, 2) the productivity procedure, and 3) the democratic procedure.[14]

The dollar procedure gives power proportionate to nominal income and is used in shareholders' meetings of firms; it dates back to the early phases of parliamentary history, when only taxpayers had voting rights. The productivity procedure distributes power proportionate to real income and is used in parliaments where not only financial capital but also human capital are represented (voting rights are based on passing an exam). This constitutes a development in a democratic direction. The democratic procedure is the one now applied in political democracies, and it has been characterized as the "least bad" procedure. Countries with the highest incomes receive the most seats under the dollar procedure, fewer seats under the productivity procedure, and still fewer under the democratic procedure.

Another option for implementing power distribution is to retain one representative for each country, but give special weight to the votes. Another is to determine the number of representatives per country proportionate to certain criteria. Yet another is to introduce two levels of voting: at the lower level, groups of countries vote and at the higher level, each group has one vote. The groups are composed in such a way that they have, as a group, the power attributed to them by the criteria chosen.

Partly as a political process and partly as a consequence of world development cooperation, the power distribution in the General Assembly will move in the same direction as in single nations: from the dollar to the productivity procedure, and from the latter to the democratic procedure. If aid to underdeveloped countries is accelerated, the democratic structure will be attained sooner than by other methods.

SUMMARY AND CONCLUSIONS

In order to attain a harmonious world community, four great problems must be solved through supranational decision-making. First, security must be achieved through disarmament to the minimum level required for deterrence. Second, the environment must be made clean and its quality maintained. Third, underdeveloped countries must be developed to eliminate the gap in economic welfare. Fourth, use of natural resources must be limited to ensure at least an equal, if not an increased, supply for future generations.

The four great problems have in common the welfare of a large number of countries. While some solutions may result from treaties between individual nations, many aspects of the four great problems require decision-making at the global level.

The United Nations provides an alternative to global treaties. The significance attached by the United States and the former Soviet Union to the United Nations is one reason why the U.N. alternative is preferred. The large powers can also be very important as initiators of activities to create solutions.

In order to implement the resolutions of the United Nations and its agencies, most of its bodies need to be reformed and strengthened. The operation of the Security Council as a peacemaking instrument requires, among other reforms, the elimination of the veto power of the permanent members. The United Nations Environment Programme needs to be given the authority to enforce its recommendations. Official development assistance to underdeveloped countries needs to increase to at least 2 percent of the donor countries' GNP. The World Bank and the International Monetary Fund must be empowered to define conditions for creditor countries that are now imposed only on debtor countries, such as the size of their contributions.

Reform of the United Nations also implies the establishment of three new specialized agencies. One is a World Treasury to collect the finances needed to operate the United Nations and to distribute contributions to member nations and agencies. Costs of financing can be reduced considerably by this method. The second new agency would be a World Police Force, permanent instead of ad hoc, which would operate in close contact with the International Court of Justice. The third new agency would be an Outer Space Agency, based on a Law of Outer Space, similar to the Law of the Sea.

As far as the timing of these reforms is concerned, those in areas where the urgency is well understood should take priority. Security reforms would come first, followed by reforms for a better environmental policy. The necessity for quicker development of underdeveloped countries is not well understood, because developed countries do not realize that it is in their own best interests to create employment in countries that currently flood them with immigrants. Still less understood are the policies needed to care for the welfare of future generations. Reforms in this area may only be possible in the long run.

In order to arrive at the optimum timing of various reforms, cost estimates should be made for solving the four great problems and carrying out the proposed reforms of U.N. institutions. The optimum timetable will be the one with the lowest total costs.

To conclude, we propose the appointment of an independent commission—an international group of experts with varied backgrounds—to evaluate the proposed reforms before the official procedure of changing the U.N. Charter begins. This commission, similar to the Brandt, Palme, and Brundtland commissions, would serve as a first step towards achieving the reforms that would revitalize the United Nations.

14 DAVID KRIEGER AND ROBERT WOETZEL
A Magna Carta for the Nuclear Age

UNIVERSAL DECLARATION OF INDIVIDUAL ACCOUNTABILITY

PREAMBLE

Affirming that all people of the world are entitled to life, liberty, and other basic human rights;

Believing that all individuals, states, and international organizations share in the responsibility to ensure peace, protect human rights, and sustain the common heritage of the planet;

Acknowledging the significant efforts of the United Nations and other international organizations toward these ends;

Committed to the United Nations Charter, the Universal Declaration of Human Rights, and the Nuremberg Principles;

Convinced that nuclear, chemical, and biological weapons have no place in a civilized world order;

Further convinced that survival in the Nuclear Age requires adherence to principles of justice and the world rule of law;

Determined to establish a just, peaceful, and civilized world order in the twenty-first century,

We proclaim this **Magna Carta for the Nuclear Age.**

ARTICLE I

All individuals, including heads of state, ministers of government, industrial, scientific and military leaders, shall be held personally accountable under international law for planning, preparing, initiating, or committing the following acts:

- **Crimes against peace,** including waging a war of aggression or a war in violation of international treaties.
- **War crimes,** including deliberate attacks against civilian populations, the use of nuclear, chemical, or biological weapons, and other grave breaches of humanitarian law.
- **Crimes against humanity,** including genocide, torture, and other serious mass violations of civil, political, economic, social, and cultural rights.
- **Crimes against the environment,** including intentional spoliation of living habitats.
- **Economic crimes against a people or nation,** including slavery in all forms.
- **Terrorism, piracy, kidnapping, hostage taking,** and the training, support, or sheltering of persons engaged in such crimes.
- **Illicit trafficking in arms or narcotics** and all acts in furtherance of such crimes.
- **Covert acts to overthrow or destabilize a legitimate foreign government,** including assassination.
- **Deliberate persecution or denial of civil rights** on grounds of race, color, gender, language, religion, political, or other opinion, national or social origin, property, birth, or other status.
- **Complicity** in committing or attempts to commit any of the aforementioned acts.

ARTICLE II

The world community shall ensure the further codification of these provisions through the continuing activities of the United Nations and other international organizations, and shall ensure compliance with them by establishing and maintaining the following institutions:

- **An International Commission of Inquiry** to engage in fact-finding and certification of cases for trial;
- **An International Criminal Court** composed of distinguished jurists, to try cases certified by the International Commission of Inquiry;
- **International Police Forces** to enforce the orders of the International Criminal Court;
- **An International Criminal Penitentiary** for confinement of convicted offenders; and
- **A Center for the Advancement of International Criminal Law and Justice,** independent of governments, to assist in codification of international criminal law and to monitor the implementation of this charter.

ARTICLE III

These provisions, upon adoption, may be added to, abridged, or altered by the common consent of the world community of nations and peoples, but without amendment they shall be binding in perpetuity.

Sovereignty must not serve as a shield to protect leaders who violate international law. Throughout history the transgressions of leaders have resulted in the death and suffering of hundreds of millions of innocent victims. In the twentieth century alone some 187 million persons have died as a result of purges, genocide, and aggressive warfare.[1] These deaths have resulted not from random acts of violence, but from official acts of government leaders.

The Nuclear Age has witnessed the scientific and technological development of weapons capable of "omnicide," the destruction of all.[2] Such powerful weapons of destruction demand controls on those who control the weapons. Thus, heads of state and government leaders must be held personally accountable for crimes committed under international law.

The Nuclear Age calls for a new way of viewing the responsibilities of citizenship and leadership. A new social pact is needed between citizens and leaders that balances rights with responsibilities and holds all individuals, regardless of position or station in life, accountable for criminal transgressions of international law. In this spirit, we call for the adoption of a Magna Carta for the Nuclear Age, with a Universal Declaration of Individual Accountability and the establishment of an International Criminal Court.

A Magna Carta is a "great charter." It provides both a turning point and a definition to a historical period. The original Magna Carta, forced on King John of England by his barons in 1215, placed the king under the rule of law and granted certain rights to the aristocracy. The original Magna Carta did little for the common man, but it foreshadowed constitutional government and democracy by subjecting the sovereign to the law.

Today we are in need of a new Magna Carta, one that is responsive to the conditions of sovereignty in the Nuclear Age. A Magna Carta for our time must take account of the fact that we now live in an interdependent world in which all borders are permeable. Nuclear weapons and other weapons of mass destruction respect no borders and threaten the survival of all life. The use of these weapons is prohibited by international law under all circumstances.[3]

The Earth, the oceans, and the atmosphere are all vulnerable to the destructive potential of improperly controlled and managed technologies.[4] No nation or leader has the right to destroy the Earth's common resources or to pollute the planet in such a way as to destroy the environment, undermine human health, and foreclose the future. A Magna Carta for the Nuclear Age must subject all nations and all individuals to the rule of international law, just as the original Magna Carta subjected King John to the rule of law. As we conceive it, the Magna Carta for the Nuclear Age is a statement of rights, responsibilities, and accountability of all individuals and nations under international law. The basic principles of the international order of the twenty-first century are spelled out in four major documents. These documents, taken together, comprise the Magna Carta for the Nuclear Age.

The first document is the United Nations Charter, which provides the legal framework and institutional structure for security and cooperation in the post-World War II period. This treaty, adopted on June 26, 1945, is now in need of revision if the United Nations Organization is to fulfill its lofty and important goals of providing for common security and preventing the scourge of war.[5]

The second of the four major documents is the Universal Declaration of Human Rights, which outlines the rights to which all individuals are entitled vis-á-vis their governments. The Universal Declaration of Human Rights was a first order of business of the newly formed United Nations General Assembly and was adopted by the General Assembly on December 10, 1948. The Universal Declaration has since been followed by implementing covenants: the International Covenant on Civil and Political Rights and the International Covenant on Economic, Social and Cultural Rights. It has also been followed by other treaties and resolutions declaring additional rights and expanding existing rights.

The third of the major documents is the Nuremberg Principles, which outlaw crimes against peace, crimes against humanity, and war crimes, and states that neither "superior orders" nor "acts of State" shall constitute a legally sufficient excuse for the commission of these crimes. The Nuremberg Principles were developed by the International Law Commission of the United Nations and adopted by the United Nations General Assembly in 1950. They are based upon the Nuremberg Charter adopted by the London Agreement on August 8, 1945, and the decisions of the International Military Tribunals, which tried German and Japanese war criminals following World War II.

The fourth document, a Universal Declaration of Individual Accountability, is more recent and has not yet been adopted by the world community. This document has been developed by the Nuclear Age Peace Foundation and the Foundation for the Establishment of an International Criminal Court. The document calls for all individuals, including heads of state and ministers of government, to be held accountable for crimes under international law. It also calls for the establishment of an International Criminal Court and other institutions necessary to enforce international law. The jurisdiction of the currently existing International Court of Justice is limited to disputes between nations and advisory opinions for the United Nations and its specialized agencies. The International Criminal Court, by contrast, would have jurisdiction over all individuals who commit major violations of international law as defined in Article I of the Universal Declaration of Individual Accountability and its eventual supporting codification.

THE UNIVERSAL DECLARATION OF INDIVIDUAL ACCOUNTABILITY

The Universal Declaration of Individual Accountability has been the critical missing element in the creation of a Magna Carta for the Nuclear Age. It replaces the guiding principle of state sovereignty, which has provided the foundation for international order for over four centuries, with an emphasis on the individual as the subject as well as the object of international law. The individual is seen as the holder of rights to be enforced against all violators of those rights; the individual is also conceived of as responsible when his or her actions violate international law and, consequently, as accountable under international law.

Under the Universal Declaration of Individual Accountability, leader and follower, rich and poor, are forewarned that certain rules apply to all alike and that no one, however powerful, shall escape the consequences of his or her actions. In the Nuclear Age we are all citizens of the world, regardless of our national affiliations, and we must accept the rights and responsibilities that are attached. As the original

Magna Carta expanded the rights of the aristocracy and increased the accountability of the king, the Magna Carta for the Nuclear Age expands the rights and responsibilities of all individuals and provides that all individuals—including those acting in official governmental capacities—shall be held accountable for criminal violations of international law.

Without the Universal Declaration of Individual Accountability, there will be no enforcement mechanism to assure that the United Nations Charter, the Universal Declaration of Human Rights and its supporting covenants, and the Nuremberg Principles and other critical standards of international law are upheld. It is thus the key element to completing the Magna Carta for the Nuclear Age, and its implementation by the world community is urgently needed.

The Universal Declaration of Individual Accountability is divided into four sections: the Preamble provides the basic principles upon which the declaration is based; Article I outlines the international criminal activities for which all individuals will be held accountable; Article II outlines the institutional structure to be established by the world community to support and enforce the provisions of Article I; and Article III makes the provisions of the declaration binding in perpetuity upon adoption. The specific provisions of the document are discussed in the sections that follow.

THE PREAMBLE

Affirming that all people of the world are entitled to life, liberty, and other basic human rights
This basic provision takes its inspiration from the U.S. Declaration of Independence. It has become axiomatic that all individuals are born with certain inalienable rights. The right to "life, liberty and security of person" is confirmed in Article 3 of the Universal Declaration of Human Rights. Other freedoms and liberties found in the Universal Declaration of Human Rights include the right to freedom of movement (Article 13), asylum from persecution (Article 14), right to marry and to found a family (Article 16), right to freedom of thought, conscience, and religion (Article 18), right to freedom of opinion and expression (Article 19), and right to peaceful assembly and association

(Article 20). The Universal Declaration also prohibits slavery or servitude (Article 4) and torture (Article 5), and provides a "right to a standard of living adequate for the health and well-being" of all individuals (Article 25). In Article 28, the Universal Declaration states that "everyone is entitled to a social and international order in which the rights and freedoms set forth in this Declaration can be fully realized."

Believing that all individuals, states, and international organizations share in the responsibility to ensure peace, protect human rights, and sustain the common heritage of the planet

Along with rights come responsibilities. They are two sides of a coin. One cannot exist without the other. The responsibility to ensure peace, protect human rights, and sustain the common heritage of the planet resides with each of us.[6] In the Nuclear Age we must act responsibly toward one another as individuals. States must also act responsibly, refraining from policies that threaten peace, violate or undermine human rights, or pollute or destroy the ecology of the planet. A grave violation of human rights and endangerment of peace is the threat or actual use of nuclear weapons or other weapons of mass destruction.

Acknowledging the significant efforts of the United Nations and other international organizations toward these ends

The United Nations and its specialized agencies have been active since the organization's inception in attempting to ensure peace, protect human rights, and sustain the common heritage of the planet. The Magna Carta for the Nuclear Age exists against the backdrop of considerable effort by the United Nations and other international organizations to achieve these goals. What has been missing in the structure of the United Nations is the implementation of a system of accountability for individuals who commit crimes under international law. Without accountability, as originally conceived in the Nuremberg Charter for crimes against peace, crimes against humanity, and war crimes, individuals acting on their own authority or under state authority will continue to threaten the peace, violate human rights, and despoil the planet.

The United Nations Organization is the vehicle for the realization of individual human aspirations. The international community must recognize, however, that if the United Nations is to succeed in its crucial mission of protecting humanity from the great threats that we face, a system of individual accountability under international law must be established. Nothing less will suffice if we are to survive the threats of nuclear "omnicide," environmental and human disasters like Chernobyl, and repeated genocidal holocausts from Auschwitz to the Iraqi attacks against the Kurds, ordered and directed by unscrupulous leaders from Hitler to Hussein.

Committed to the United Nations Charter, The Universal Declaration of Human Rights, and the Nuremberg Principles
As already stated, these are the basic documents that form the foundation of the Magna Carta for the Nuclear Age. They established the framework for individual and state action in the post-World War II period, having emerged from the ashes of that war. The potential of these instruments was blunted by the Cold War, with its emphasis on threat and counter-threat and its accompanying nuclear arms race. We now stand at a historical juncture where the Cold War has ended, and these instruments may again provide a basis for regulating rights and enforcing responsibilities under international law. Unfortunately, these documents are not widely known or understood. Effective citizenship in the Nuclear Age is dependent upon an understanding of the rights and responsibilities established by these documents. The Universal Declaration of Individual Accountability builds upon and reinforces the principles provided for in these critically important documents.

Convinced that nuclear, chemical, and biological weapons have no place in a civilized world order
Nuclear, chemical, and biological weapons are all weapons of mass destruction. They are weapons of total annihilation, killing indiscriminately soldiers and civilians, men, women, and children. They are not weapons of combat, but of cowards. All are outlawed by international treaties and the law of civilized nations. And yet, nations continue to

design, develop, test, manufacture, stockpile, deploy, threaten to use, and use these weapons; and these activities are carried out by individuals within nations. Before greater crimes are committed, these weapons must be dismantled under a well-designed system of international verification. Those nations and individuals refusing to cooperate in the dismantling of these weapons of mass destruction must be brought before an International Criminal Court and tried for the planning and preparation of crimes against humanity.

Further convinced that survival in the Nuclear Age requires adherence to principles of justice and the world rule of law
The predominant characteristic of the Nuclear Age is the threat of mass annihilation in which our "advances" in destructive technology have placed the survival of the human species in jeopardy. For the first time in human evolution it is possible to imagine the annihilation of humankind. Only by applying principles of justice and the rule of law will it be possible to control the omnicidal weaponry we have created.

We are aware that the nuclear genie is out of the bottle, and without strict international controls on nuclear materials there will come a day when the have-not nations of the world and terrorist leaders have the capacity to threaten nuclear holocausts. To prevent this day from occurring, we must recognize that peace on our increasingly interdependent globe requires that every individual's needs on the planet be dealt with justly. As Adlai Stevenson pointed out with great eloquence, we cannot continue to exist on "Spaceship Earth" with a small portion of the crew living in abundance while the vast majority live in crushing poverty. Without justice there can be no peace; without peace there can be no assured future for humankind; without adherence to international law both peace and justice stand in jeopardy.

Determined to establish a just, peaceful, and civilized world order in the twenty-first century
As we stand on the brink of a new century and a new millennium, it is appropriate to keep in mind that human existence on Earth is but a fraction of a second in geological time. In our short history on Earth,

our accomplishments as a species have been dramatic. The human genius and capacity for creativity are boundless. We now stand threatened by that very genius and creativity turned to destructive ends. If we are to survive and prosper as a species we must focus our attention on the constructive goal of creating a just and peaceful world order in the twenty-first century.

We have lived long enough under the sword of Damocles. It is time for humanity to emerge from the burden of threat and destruction that has thus far characterized the Nuclear Age and to assert our claim to a just and peaceful world order. The new world order must be one that honors the dignity and worth of every individual, that respects the legacies of all peoples—their identities, ethnicities, cultures, and, above all, their diversity. In our diverse human heritage lies the seeds of greatness. If we are to nurture this greatness in future generations, we must provide the soil in which these seeds can take root. We will do this by creating and strengthening the institutions necessary for a just and peaceful world order. Among these institutions, an International Criminal Court will be necessary to hold in check the destructive potential of individual leaders.

The Universal Declaration of Individual Accountability provides a critical new element in the Magna Carta for the Nuclear Age. This element is accountability of all individuals under international law. The document is especially for leaders who would place in jeopardy the survival of our species by criminal acts in violation of international law. The same principles of responsibility and accountability laid down at Nuremberg must now be expanded and implemented on an international and impartial basis to assure a world order in the twenty-first century that values and supports human dignity and defends all life. This is a world order worthy of the promise, intelligence, and creativity of humankind.

ARTICLE I

All individuals, including heads of state, ministers of government, and industrial, scientific and military leaders, shall be held personally accountable under international law for planning, preparing, initiating, or committing the following acts.

This article sets forth the primary proposition of the Universal Declaration of Individual Accountability: all individuals, regardless of position or station in life, shall be held accountable for criminal acts in violation of international law. This is in keeping with the position taken by U.S. Supreme Court Justice Robert Jackson, the chief Nuremberg prosecutor, who said in his opening statement at Nuremberg that the "principle of personal liability is a necessary and logical one if international law is to render real help in the maintenance of peace." Justice Jackson assured the world "that while this law is first applied against German aggressors, the law includes, and if it is to serve a useful purpose it must condemn aggression by any other nations, including those which sit here now in judgment." [7]

Within all nations, individuals are held accountable for criminal violations of national law. Without such accountability, the law within nations would be ineffectual and unenforceable. A lack of individual accountability currently exists at the international level. If we are to create a just world order ruled by law rather than the force of arms, then the principle of individual accountability must be recognized and applied in international law.

The International Law Commission (ILC), established by the U.N. General Assembly in 1947, was charged with preparation of a Draft Code of Crimes Against the Peace and Security of Mankind ("Draft Code") taking into account the principles of international law recognized in the Charter of the Nuremberg Tribunal and the Judgment of the Tribunal. The Draft Code, provisionally adopted by the ILC on July 12, 1991, states that "an individual who commits a crime against the peace and security of mankind is responsible therefor and liable to punishment" (Article 3(1)). The Draft Code further states that "The official position of an individual who commits a crime against the peace and security of mankind, and particularly the fact that he acts as Head of State or Government, does not relieve him of criminal responsibility" (Article 13).

In discussing specific Article I crimes, we will refer to the applicable provisions of the Draft Code as provisionally adopted by the ILC.

Crimes against peace, including waging a war of aggression or a war in violation of international treaties.

Article 2(4) of the United Nations Charter provides that "All members shall refrain in their international relations from the threat or use of force against the territorial integrity or political independence of any state, or in any other manner inconsistent with the Purposes of the United Nations."

Crimes against peace were clearly articulated in Nuremberg Principle VI(2)(a), which set out the following acts as punishable under international law:

(i) Planning, preparation, initiation or waging of a war of aggression or a war in violation of international treaties, agreements or assurances;

(ii) Participation in a common plan or conspiracy for the accomplishment of any of the acts mentioned under (i)."

On December 14, 1974, the U.N. General Assembly, after many years of work, agreed upon a Definition of Aggression. The definition included the following acts:

(a) The invasion or attack by the armed forces of a State on the territory of another State, or any military occupation, however temporary, resulting from such invasion or attack, or any annexation by the use of force of the territory of another State or part thereof;

(b) Bombardment by the armed forces of a State against the territory of another State or the use of any weapons by a State against the territory of another State;

(c) The blockade of the ports or coasts of a State by the armed forces of another State;

(d) An attack by the armed forces of a State on the land, sea or air forces, or marine and air fleets of another State;

(e) The use of armed forces of one State which are within the territory of another State with the agreement of the receiving State, in contravention of the conditions provided for in the agreement or any extension of their presence in such territory beyond the termination of the agreement;

(f) The action of a State in allowing its territory, which it has placed at the disposal of another State, to be used by that other State for perpetrating an act of aggression against a third State;

(g) The sending by or on behalf of a State of armed bands, groups, irregulars or mercenaries, which carry out acts of armed force against another State of such gravity as to amount to the acts listed above, or its substantial involvement therein.

In Article 5 of the Definition of Aggression, the General Assembly stated:

1. No consideration of whatever nature, whether political, economic, military or otherwise, may serve as a justification for aggression.

2. A war of aggression is a crime against international peace. Aggression gives rise to international responsibility.

3. No territorial acquisition or special advantage resulting from aggression is or shall be recognized as lawful.

The Draft Code of Crimes Against the Peace and Security of Mankind has designated "Aggression" (Article 15) and "Threat of Aggression" (Article 16) as crimes under international law. The Draft Code states in Article 15(2), "Aggression is the use of armed force by a State against the sovereignty, territorial integrity or political independence of another State, or in any other manner inconsistent with the Charter of the United Nations." Article 15 gives numerous specific examples of aggressive acts. Article 16(2) defines Threat of Aggression as "declarations, communications, demonstrations of force or any other measures which would give good reason to the Government of a State to believe that aggression is being seriously contemplated against that State."

Elie Wiesel, Nobel Peace Laureate and survivor of World War II concentration camps, has stated before the U.S. Senate Foreign Relations Committee:

Let history record our determination that whenever an aggressor will launch war against defenseless countries, his story will inexorably lead him before an international court of justice. His sentence will almost be irrelevant. His personal future will matter little. What will matter is the exposure of his criminal deeds. What will matter is that he will remain in the annals of history as an example of what human beings, driven by fanaticism or ambition, can do to one another.[8]

War crimes, including deliberate attacks against civilian populations, the use of nuclear, chemical, or biological weapons, and other grave breaches of humanitarian law.

Modern limitations on conduct in warfare go back to the Declaration of St. Petersburg, in which the contracting parties agreed on December 11, 1868, "mutually to renounce, in case of war among themselves, the employment by their military or naval troops of any projectile of a weight below 400 grammes, which is either explosive or charged with fulminating or inflammable substances."

War crimes were elaborated in the Hague Conventions of 1899 and 1907 and the Geneva Conventions of 1949 and the Additional Protocols thereto. The four Geneva Conventions adopted on August 12, 1949, are:

   I. Geneva Convention for the Amelioration of the Condition of the Wounded and Sick in Armed Forces in the Field;

  II. Geneva Convention for the Amelioration of the Condition of Wounded, Sick and Shipwrecked Members of Armed Forces at Sea;

III. Geneva Convention relative to the Treatment of Prisoners of War; and

IV. Geneva Convention relative to the Protection of Civilian Persons in Time of War.

The Additional Protocols to the Geneva Conventions done on June 10, 1977, provide *inter alia* the following basic rules:

  1.In any armed conflict, the right of the Parties to the conflict to choose methods or means of warfare is not unlimited.

2. It is prohibited to employ weapons, projectiles and materials and methods of warfare of a nature to cause superfluous injury or unnecessary suffering.

3. It is prohibited to employ methods or means of warfare which are intended, or may be expected, to cause widespread, long-term and severe damage to the natural environment (Article 35).

In order to ensure respect for and protection of the civilian population and civilian objects, the Parties to the conflict shall at all times distinguish between the civilian population and combatants and between civilian objects and military objectives and accordingly shall direct their operations only against military objectives (Article 48).

Nuremberg Principle VI(2)(b) provides for individual accountability for the following war crimes:

Violations of the laws or customs of war which include, but are not limited to, murder, ill-treatment or deportation to slave-labour or for any other purpose of civilian population of or in occupied territory, murder or ill-treatment of prisoners of war or persons on the seas, killing of hostages, plunder of public or private property, wanton destruction of cities, towns, or villages, or devastation not justified by military necessity.

On November 11, 1970 a United Nations Convention on the Non-Applicability of Statutory Limitations to War Crimes and Crimes Against Humanity entered into force. The convention defines war crimes in Article I "as they are defined in the Charter of the International Military Tribunal, Nurnberg, of 8 August 1945 and confirmed by resolutions 3(I) of 13 February 1946 and 95(I) of 11 December 1946 of the General Assembly of the United Nations, particularly the 'grave breaches' enumerated in the Geneva Conventions of 12 August 1949 for the protection of war victims."

Article II of the convention makes the provisions of the treaty applicable to "*representatives of State authority and private individuals* who as principals or accomplices, participate in or who directly incite others" to Article I crimes. (Emphasis added.)

The Draft Code of Crimes Against the Peace and Security of Mankind specifies as criminal conduct committing or ordering the commission of an exceptionally serious war crime (Article 22(1)). Such crimes are defined in Article 22(2) as "exceptionally serious violations of principles and rules of international law applicable in armed conflict consisting of any of the following acts:

  (a) acts of inhumanity, cruelty or barbarity directed against the life, dignity or physical or mental integrity of persons [in particular willful killing, torture, mutilation, taking of hostages, deportation or transfer of civilian population and collective punishment];
  (b) use of unlawful weapons;
  (c) employing methods or means of warfare which are intended or may be expected to cause widespread, long-term and severe damage to the natural environment;
  (d) large-scale destruction of civilian property;
  (e) willful attacks on property of exceptional religious, historical or cultural value.

Crimes against humanity, including genocide, torture, and other serious mass violations of civil, political, economic, social, and cultural rights.

Crimes Against Humanity were articulated in Article VI(2)(c) of the Nuremberg Principles to include:

  Murder, extermination, enslavement, deportation and other inhuman acts done against any civilian population, or persecutions on political, racial or religious grounds, when such acts are done or such persecutions are carried on in execution of or in connection with any crime against peace or any war crime.

  Such crimes have been further developed under international law in the following treaties:

  • Convention on the Prevention and Punishment of the Crime of Genocide (December 9, 1948);
  • International Covenant on Civil and Political Rights (December 16, 1966);

- International Covenant on Economic, Social, and Cultural Rights (December 16, 1966);
- Convention Against Torture and Other Cruel, Inhuman or Degrading Treatment or Punishment (December 10, 1984).

The Genocide Convention states in Article IV that "Persons committing Genocide . . . shall be punished, *whether they are constitutionally responsible rulers, public officials or private individuals.*" (Emphasis added.)

Crimes Against Humanity, whether committed in time of war or peace, are defined in the Convention on the Non-applicability of Statutory Limitations to War Crimes and Crimes Against Humanity "as they are defined in the Charter of the International Military Tribunal, Nurnberg, of 8 August 1945 and confirmed by resolutions 3(I) of 13 February 1946 and 95(I) of 11 December 1946 of the General Assembly of the United Nations, eviction by armed attack or occupation and inhuman acts resulting from the policy of apartheid, and the crime of genocide as defined in the 1948 Convention on the Prevention and Punishment of the Crime of Genocide, *even if such acts do not constitute a violation of the domestic law of the country in which they are committed.*" (Emphasis added.)

The Draft Code seeks to hold accountable any individual "who commits or orders the commission by another individual of an act of genocide . . ." (Article 19(1)). Genocide is defined as "any of the following acts committed with the intent to destroy, in whole or in part, a national, ethnic, racial or religious group as such:

(a) killing members of a group;

(b) causing serious bodily or mental harm to members of the group;

(c) deliberately inflicting on the group conditions of life calculated to bring about its physical destruction in whole or in part;

(d) imposing measures intended to prevent births within the group;

(e) forcibly transferring children of the group to another group (Article 19(2)).

Crimes against the environment, including intentional spoliation of living habitats.

Criminal conduct against the environment is not yet defined in the way that the three main Nuremberg crimes (crimes against peace, war crimes, and crimes against humanity) have been. Yet, it is clear that, given modern technological capabilities, conduct that affects the natural and human environment can have far-reaching consequences for humanity for countless generations to follow. Individuals must be held accountable for planning, preparing, initiating, or committing acts that would poison or otherwise destroy the Earth's environment.

The United Nations has issued several major statements on the need for environmental protection that provide a basis for developing a code of offenses against the environment. These include:
* Declaration of the United Nations Conference on the Human Environment (June 16, 1972);
* World Charter for Nature (November 9, 1982); and
* Protection of the Global Climate for Present and Future Generations of Mankind (December 21, 1990).

A U.N. Convention on the Prohibition of Military or any Other Hostile Use of Environmental Modification Techniques entered into force on October 5, 1978.

The Basel Convention on the Control of Transboundary Movements of Hazardous Wastes and Their Disposal, done at Basel on March 22, 1989, categorized the illegal traffic in hazardous wastes or other wastes as "criminal" (Article IV (3)).

The Draft Code calls for criminal accountability of "an individual who wilfully causes or orders another individual to cause widespread, long-term and severe damage to the natural environment . . ." (Article 26).

Economic crimes against a people or nation, including slavery in all forms.

Economic crimes against a people or nation, with the exception of slavery, remain largely to be defined by the international community. Slavery was made criminal by the Convention on the Prohibition of Slavery (September 7, 1956).

Guidelines for developing a code of offenses for Economic Crimes may be found in the U.N. Declaration on the Right to Development (December 4, 1986) and in a "Magna Carta for International Economic Development, Rights and Responsibilities" published by the Foundation for the Establishment of an International Criminal Court in 1989.[9]

The Draft Code seeks criminal accountability for "an individual who as leader or organizer establishes or maintains by force, colonial domination or any other form of alien domination contrary to the rights of peoples to self-determination as enshrined in the Charter of the United Nations . . . " (Article 18).

Terrorism, piracy, kidnapping, hostage taking, and the training, support, or sheltering of persons engaged in such crimes.
A series of international conventions prohibit these acts and provide for criminal sanctions. The common theme of these conventions is to protect innocent persons from attack by those who would use such attacks to send a message or to punish others.

These conventions include:

- Convention on Offenses and Certain Other Acts Committed on Board Aircraft, signed at Tokyo on September 14, 1963;
- Convention for the Suppression of Unlawful Seizure of Aircraft, signed at The Hague on December 16, 1970;
- Convention for the Suppression of Unlawful Acts against the Safety of Civil Aviation, concluded at Montreal on September 23, 1971;
- Convention on the Prevention and Punishment of Crimes against Internationally Protected Persons, including Diplomatic Agents, adopted at New York on December 14, 1973;
- International Convention against the Taking of Hostages, adopted in New York on December 17, 1979;
- Convention on the Physical Protection of Nuclear Material, adopted at Vienna on March 3, 1980;

- Protocol for the Suppression of Unlawful Acts of Violence at Airports Serving International Civil Aviation, Supplementary to the Convention for the Suppression of Unlawful Acts against the Safety of Civil Aviation, done at Montreal on February 24, 1988;
- Convention for the Suppression of Unlawful Acts against the Safety of Maritime Navigation, signed at Rome on March 10, 1988;
- Protocol for the Suppression of Unlawful Acts against the Safety of Fixed Platforms located on the Continental Shelf, signed at Rome on March 10, 1988.

The U.N. General Assembly stated on December 4, 1989, that it "once again unequivocally condemns, *as criminal and unjustifiable*, all acts, methods and practices of terrorism wherever and by whomever committed. . . . " (Resolution adopted in Report of Sixth Committee 44/29, emphasis added.)

International terrorism is defined in the Draft Code as "undertaking, organizing, assisting, financing, encouraging or tolerating acts against another State directed at persons or property and of such a nature as to create a state of terror in the minds of public figures, groups of persons or the general public" (Article 24).

Illicit trafficking in arms or narcotics, and all acts in furtherance of such crimes.

Article 26 of the United Nations Charter provides:

In order to promote the establishment and maintenance of international peace and security with the least diversion for armaments of the world's human and economic resources, the Security Council shall be responsible for formulating, with the assistance of the Military Staff Committee referred to in Article 47, plans to be submitted to the Members of the United Nations *for the establishment of a system for the regulation of armaments.* (Emphasis added.)

As yet, however, a system for the regulation of armaments required by Article 26 has not been developed, and the arms trade continues unchecked. This is an area in great need of regulation with appropriate criminal sanctions, and the United Nations should move rapidly to achieve this end.

A United Nations Convention Against Illicit Traffic in Narcotic Drugs and Psychotropic Substances was adopted on December 19, 1988. This Convention calls in Article 3 for each Party *"to adopt such measures as may be necessary to establish as criminal offenses"* a wide range of activities connected with drug trafficking including "production, manufacture, extraction, preparation, offering, offering for sale, distribution for sale, delivery on any terms whatsoever, brokerage, dispatch, dispatch in transit, transport, importation or exportation of such narcotic drug or any psychotropic substance. . . . " (Emphasis added.)

Having recognized these and other activities in furtherance of narcotic trafficking to be criminal acts, the next step is to provide for international jurisdiction over such acts when domestic courts do not assert jurisdiction.

The Draft Code defines as criminal acts the commission or ordering the commission of "undertaking, organizing, facilitating, financing or encouraging of illicit traffic in narcotic drugs on a large scale, whether within the confines of a State or in a transboundary context" (Article 25(1)).

Covert acts to overthrow or destabilize a legitimate foreign government, including assassination.
If the world is to set the rule of law above the rule of force, then covert acts to overthrow or destabilize legitimate foreign governments, including assassination, must not be allowed. This raises the question of whether the international community is helpless in dealing with a tyrant who comes to power by legitimate means. The answer is no. This situation may be dealt with by bringing the tyrant before an International Criminal Court for whatever offenses have been committed or attempted. If the tyrant will not appear, he could be tried in absentia. Upon conviction by the International Criminal Court, an individual who continues to serve as head of state or head of government would cause the legitimacy of the government to be withdrawn by the world

community. The convicted tyrant would be subject to apprehension by the citizens of his nation or by international forces.

The Draft Code provides criminal sanctions for Intervention ("in the internal or external affairs of a State"), which is defined as "fomenting [armed] subversion or terrorist activities or by organizing, assisting or financing such activities, or supplying arms for the purpose of such activities, thereby [seriously] undermining the free exercise by that State of its sovereign rights" (Article 17(2)).

Deliberate persecution or denial of civil rights on grounds of race, color, gender, language, religion, political or other opinion, national or social origin, property, birth or other status.
Article 1 of the Universal Declaration of Human Rights states that "all human beings are born free and equal in dignity and rights. They are endowed with reason and conscience and should act toward one another in a spirit of brotherhood."

The following international conventions pertain to criminal conduct in this area:

- International Convention on the Suppression and Punishment of the Crime of Apartheid, adopted on November 30, 1973;
- International Covenant on Civil and Political Rights, adopted on December 16, 1966;
- International Covenant on Economic, Social and Cultural Rights, adopted on December 16, 1966;
- Convention on the Elimination of all forms of Racial Discrimination, adopted on December 21, 1965; and
- Convention on the Rights of the Child, adopted on November 20, 1989.

The International Convention on the Suppression and Punishment of the Crime of Apartheid states in Article I(1) that "*apartheid is a crime against humanity* and that inhuman acts resulting from the policies and practices of *apartheid* and similar policies and practices of racial segregation and discrimination... *are crimes violating principles of international law,* in particular the purposes and principles of the Charter of the United Nations, and constituting a serious threat to international peace and security." Article I(2) states, "The States Parties to the Present Convention *declare criminal those organizations, institutions and individuals committing the crime of apartheid.*" (Emphasis added.)

The convention further provides in Article III that "*International criminal responsibility shall apply*, irrespective of the motive involved, *to individuals, members of organizations and institutions and representatives of the State. . . .*" (Emphasis added.)

It is clear that the world community intended that criminal responsibility attach to the commission of the crime of apartheid. With criminal responsibility must come accountability under international law for one's acts.

The Draft Code seeks to hold accountable individuals who commit or order the commission of "Systematic or mass violations of human rights, consisting of:

(a) murder;

(b) torture;

(c) establishing or maintaining over persons a status of slavery, servitude or forced labour;

(d) deportation or forcible transfer of population;

(e) persecution on social, political, racial, religious or cultural grounds (Article 21).

Complicity in committing or attempts to commit any of the aforementioned acts.

Those who participate in international criminal activities, either directly or indirectly, should be held accountable for their acts. This section allows for the assertion of jurisdiction over individuals who aid or abet in committing or who unsuccessfully attempt to commit the previously discussed crimes.

The Draft Code, in Article 3(2), provides penalties for any "individual who aids, abets or provides the means for the commission of a crime against the peace and security of mankind or conspires in or directly incites the commission of such a crime. . . ."

In Article 3(3) the Draft Code seeks to hold accountable individuals who attempt to commit a crime against the peace and security of mankind. Attempt is defined as "any commencement of execution of a crime that failed or was halted only because of circumstances independent of the perpetrator's intention."

ARTICLE II

The world community shall ensure the further codification of these provisions through the continuing activities of the United Nations and other international organizations, and shall ensure compliance with them by establishing and maintaining the following institutions.

It has been more than four decades since the International Law Commission began its work on preparing a Draft Code of Crimes Against the Peace and Security of Mankind. The necessary steps must now be taken for the world community acting through the United Nations to adopt the code. While the code may not be complete or perfect at the outset, it should be adopted and then expanded or amended as appropriate.

If law is to be effective it must have some method of enforcement. This is as true of international law as of national law. The institutions necessary to enforce international law will require some transfer of sovereignty from the national to the international level. This transfer has already taken place in many areas where supranational decision-making is required, including the various organs and specialized agencies of the United Nations. Now it needs to occur in the area of international criminal law.

An International Commission of Inquiry to engage in fact-finding and certification of cases for trial

The International Commission of Inquiry (ICI) would be similar to a grand jury. It would be composed of an impartial group of jurists who would investigate and evaluate complaints against individuals for violations of Article I provisions. The ICI would be charged with certifying a case for trial, recommending against trial, or suggesting an alternate disposition of the case.

An International Criminal Court, composed of distinguished jurists, to try cases certified by the International Commission of Inquiry

The International Criminal Court (ICC) would exercise jurisdiction over all cases certified by the ICI. It would be composed of impartial and distinguished jurists, chosen in their expert capacity and representative of the world community. The court would be responsible for assuring that defendants' basic rights are protected including, *inter alia*, the right to be considered innocent until proven guilty beyond a reasonable doubt, the right to competent counsel, the right against self-incrimination.

The Draft Code of Crimes Against the Peace and Security of Mankind provides for "the minimum guarantees due to all human beings with regard to the law and the facts," including "the right to be presumed innocent until proven guilty." The following rights are also proposed in the Draft Code:

(a) in the determination of any charge against him, to have a fair and public hearing by a competent, independent and impartial tribunal duly established by law or by treaty;

(b) to be informed promptly and in detail in a language which he understands of the nature and cause of the charge against him;

(c) to have adequate time and facilities for the preparation of his defence and to communicate with counsel of his own choosing;

(d) to be tried without undue delay;

(e) to be tried in his presence, and to defend himself in person or through legal assistance of his own choosing; to be informed, if he does not have legal assistance, of this right; and to have legal assistance assigned to him and without payment by him in any such case if he does not have sufficient means to pay for it;

(f) to examine, or have examined, the witnesses against him and to obtain the attendance and examination of witnesses on his behalf under the same conditions as witnesses against him;

(g) to have the free assistance of an interpreter if he cannot understand or speak the language used in court;

(h) not to be compelled to testify against himself or to confess guilt (Article 8).

International Police Forces to enforce the orders of the International Criminal Court
International Police Forces would support the ICC with regard to the control of criminal proceedings and the incarceration of criminals. International Police Forces are not conceived of as invasion forces capable of apprehending noncooperating defendants. The court would rely upon national police forces to aid it in this function when necessary.

An International Criminal Penitentiary for confinement of convicted offenders
The function of confining convicted offenders would be fulfilled by an International Criminal Penitentiary. The prison at Spandau that housed German war criminals convicted by the International Military Tribunals following World War II provides an example.

A Center for the Advancement of International Criminal Law and Justice, independent of governments, to assist in codification of international criminal law and monitoring the implementation of this charter.
The institutions previously discussed would be international organizations composed of international civil servants. These institutions would be official international bodies given legitimacy and supported financially by nations. The Center for the Advancement of International Criminal Law and Justice would, however, be independent of governments. It would be composed of nongovernmental representatives, and would serve to support and monitor the implementation of the Universal Declaration of Individual Accountability.

ARTICLE III

These provisions upon adoption, may be added to, abridged or altered by the common consent of the world community of nations and peoples, but without amendment they shall be binding in perpetuity.
This article allows that, upon adoption, the Universal Declaration of Individual Accountability is subject to amendment by the world community. Without amendment, the provisions will bind all signatories in perpetuity.

CONCLUSION

If we are to preserve the human rights achieved so painfully in our century, we must accept responsibility for protecting those rights and impose accountability on all individuals, regardless of their office, who violate those rights guaranteed under international law.

As technological advances have made the world smaller, we can no longer tolerate the exercise of sovereignty in violation of international law. The prerogatives of sovereignty must end where the rights of other nations and peoples begin. No sovereign nation or national leader, acting with or without state authority, can be allowed to trample on the rights of other nations or peoples. Nor can nations and national leaders be allowed to destroy the Earth's common resources or to endanger peace in the name of sovereignty. To prevent such transgressions, it serves the ends of justice to impose individual accountability under international law.

The Magna Carta for the Nuclear Age brings the Nuremberg Principles into the Nuclear Age and places sovereignty into the proper perspective for the twenty-first century by recognizing that:

(1) international law is necessary to ensure peace, protect human rights and sustain the common heritage of the planet;

(2) no nation or national leader stands above international law; and

(3) individual accountability under international law requires an institutional framework to include the establishment of an International Criminal Court.

The twentieth century has been witness to unthinkable brutality and horror. In World War II alone some 50 million persons were killed. Since World War II there have been some 130 wars, killing some 20 million persons. In all, over 100 million persons have died in wars during this century. If the implementation of the Universal Declaration of Individual Accountability were to prevent just one future war or stop one future Hitler, Stalin, or Hussein, it would justify its establishment.

The Universal Declaration of Individual Accountability places its emphasis on enforcement of a system of criminal justice at the global level. As with any system of criminal justice, however, it is motivated more by the desire to protect the innocent than to punish the guilty. In the case of the most serious international crimes, the innocent can include whole cities, even entire nations or peoples, and the innocent may encompass future generations still unborn.

The Magna Carta for the Nuclear Age would not impinge upon current international law as it applies to states. It would simply add the new and critical element of individual accountability under international law. The International Court of Justice will remain available for judicial settlement of disputes between nations. The International Criminal Court will be established under the Magna Carta for the exclusive purpose of taking jurisdiction over individuals who commit grave criminal violations of international law.

The Magna Carta for the Nuclear Age is a proposal for action by the world community. Its implementation during this United Nations Decade of International Law would represent an important step toward achieving a just, peaceful, and civilized world order in the twenty-first century, a world order respectful of human dignity and the uniqueness of life.

15 | DAVID KRIEGER
Earth Citizenship

In an earlier age security required shifting from a feudal to a national identity. Today security requires a shift in identity from the nation to the Earth. The castle, once impregnable, became vulnerable to new technologies of attack. Security demanded not thicker castle walls, nor a wider moat, but a new form of social and political organization— the nation. Today, the "castle walls" surrounding nations have become vulnerable, and nations have tried to shore up their sagging "defenses" with new and ever-more-powerful weapons of mass destruction with which they threaten retaliation. However, this approach to security simply increases the danger of global annihilation and cannot preserve national security any more than thicker castle walls could preserve the feudal system.

The dangers that confront humanity have brought us to the point of requiring a conscious commitment to Earth Citizenship if we are to save our endangered planet. Regardless of one's background, or one's ideology, religion, race, nationality, or gender, we share a common heritage with each of the more than five billion humans who inhabit the planet. We are all citizens of Earth, whatever else we may be, and we are all capable of envisioning and creating a better future.

As we know, ours is the third planet rotating around a remote star in a remote galaxy in a vast universe that, we are told, is expanding. Of the billions of planets in our universe, we know of only one with that special combination of elements and conditions giving rise to life. We share the knowledge that on our unique planet life exists, and each of us in our own way can attest to that wonder. It is beyond our power to understand why life exists, how or when it came to be, or what its purpose may be. What is within our power is to decide whether or not we are willing to work to save and preserve our unique planet and its most valuable and precious resource, life.

The Earth is being threatened and despoiled as never before.[1] The litany of dangers and threats is well known. Powerful arsenals of nuclear weapons are poised to destroy civilization and perhaps all human life.[2] These weapons, and the governmental programs that have supported their development and deployment, have undermined our societies and subverted our militaries, our scientists, our educational institutions, our values, our democracy, and our future. Nuclear weapons are unjustifiable, even as weapons of war, since they kill indiscriminately, drawing no distinction between combatants and civilians.

However, nuclear weapons are widely believed by political and military elites to be necessary to provide security. Those who oppose nuclear weapons are often viewed as impractical, idealistic, and unpatriotic. Somehow the high ground of the debate over nuclear arsenals and strategies has been seized by political and military leaders, bureaucrats, academics, and scientists who are willing to risk the future of the planet to maintain their concept of national security and/or national interest.

George Kennan, who in his elder years has become a statesman for peace and an advocate of substantial nuclear disarmament, was the author of a 1947 State Department report that set the tone for U.S. foreign policy following World War II. Kennan wrote:

> We have about 50% of the world's wealth but only 6.3% of its population. . . . In this situation we cannot fail to be the object of envy and resentment. Our real task in the coming period is to devise a pattern of relationships which will permit us to maintain this position of disparity. . . . We should dispense with the aspiration "to be liked" or regarded as the repository of high-minded international altruism. . . . We should cease talk about vague and unreal objectives such as human rights, the raising of the living standards, and democratization. The day is not

far off when we are going to have to deal in straight power concepts. . . . [3]

The U.S. has not been alone in the development of planet-threatening nuclear arsenals. The former Soviet Union, of course, also participated in the nuclear arms race and to a lesser, but still significant, extent, so did the British, French, Chinese, and Israelis. And so, we strongly suspect, did the South Africans. And so will others, including those we fear most—irrational national leaders and fanatical terrorists—if the insanity of the nuclear arms race is not stopped by the citizens of Earth.

Other threats to the Earth, in addition to nuclear and other weapons of mass annihilation, include overpopulation; pollution of the atmosphere, oceans, rivers, and lakes by acid rain and other forms of industrial and agricultural contaminants; destruction of the ozone layer; altering of the Earth's climate; deforestation; desertification; erosion of topsoil; etc. [4]

BETTER OPTIONS

There are better options for us than nuclear devastation or environmental destruction. But these better, happier options will not come about by themselves. They will require leadership and the participation of Earth citizens around the globe. The problems are not someone else's; they are ours. But before the problems can be solved, we must understand some basic truths of our time:

- We have only one Earth;
- National borders are manmade and permeable to missiles and pollution as well as to persons and ideas;
- In the Nuclear Age, defense is no longer possible;
- Instead of defense we have substituted deterrence (which is simply a fancy name for the threat of retaliation);
- Sovereignty has become limited by the power and scope of our industrial and military technologies;
- Security in the Nuclear Age can only be common security (which means that national security can only be achieved in the context of global security);

• Global security requires appropriate global institutions and global perspective.

The astronauts and cosmonauts saw the Earth as a single, unitary whole. They recognized the uniqueness, fragility, and incredible beauty of our planet. They understood emotionally in ways that few people on Earth have grasped that our unique repository of life must be preserved against all threats.

From outer space it is clear that national borders are artificial constructs. The lines that we see on maps delineating boundaries between nations do not really exist on the Earth. These lines may seem real when we look at a map, but they are not. Borders cannot prevent the spread of pollution, the transmittal of ideas, nor missile or terrorist attacks.

Since borders are permeable, defense is not possible. However, most national leaders still talk and act as if defense were possible. In truth, however, nations cannot defend their borders against attacks by determined opponents. Instead, governments have developed a strategy known as "deterrence." Governments can no longer defend their citizens; rather they threaten retaliation against any opponent that attacks them.

There are at least three major problems with relying upon retaliation: first, it cannot prevent an attack that is launched accidentally or inadvertently; second, there are terrorists who will not be deterred by threats of retaliation; and third, retaliation by means of today's nuclear weapons of mass destruction could result in the indiscriminate killing of hundreds of millions of innocent persons.

Today's technologies transcend national control. Just as nations cannot defend against modern weapons technologies, they also cannot protect their citizens against the environmental effects of energy, transportation, and industrial technologies. No single nation can solve the problems connected with ozone depletion, climate change, acid rain, deforestation, desertification, etc.

Nations have traditionally claimed that they are sovereign, meaning that they exercise complete control over their territories. However, if borders are permeable and technology has created global problems that no single nation can solve, then we must conclude that sovereignty is now limited. This means that certain decisions affecting the welfare of our planet, and consequently the welfare of the citizens of every nation, must be made at an international or global level. In the Nuclear Age, the only effective security for the citizens of any nation is common security. We currently have an organization that is committed to achieving common security—the United Nations. The preamble to the United Nations Charter affirms a commitment "to save succeeding generations from the scourge of war. . . . " In the aftermath of the Cold War the United Nations is being empowered to provide for common security. A revitalization and restructuring of the United Nations is needed that will give it increased legislative, judicial, and enforcement powers.[5]

Nations do not make wars or commit crimes against peace or humanity—humans do. This understanding was taken into account when the war criminals were punished in International Military Tribunals after the World War II and the Principles of Nuremberg were established. These principles state that no one can violate international law, not even heads of state or heads of government, without being subject to criminal punishment. These principles should be a required element of education in the Nuclear Age.

Without a global perspective we will continue to try to solve the new and threatening problems that confront us with old solutions based on national sovereignty and military might. These solutions are doomed to failure because no one nation can protect itself or its citizens from these global threats.

THE NUREMBERG PRINCIPLES

Principle I. Any person who commits an act that constitutes a crime under international law is responsible therefor and liable to punishment.

Principle II. The fact that internal law does not impose a penalty for an act that constitutes a crime under international law does not relieve the person who committed the act from responsibility under international law.

Principle III. The fact that a person who committed an act that constitutes a crime under international law acted as head of state or responsible government official does not relieve him from responsibility under international law.

Principle IV. The fact that a person acted pursuant to order of his government or of a superior does not relieve him from responsibility under international law, provided a moral choice was in fact possible to him.

Principle V. Any person charged with a crime under international law has the right to a fair trial on the facts and law.

Principle VI. The crimes hereinafter set out are punishable as crimes under international law:

(a) *Crimes against peace:*

(i) Planning, preparation, initiation or waging of a war of aggression or a war in violation of international treaties, agreements or assurances;

(ii) Participation in a common plan or conspiracy for the accomplishment of any of the acts mentioned under (i).

(b) *War crimes:*

Violations of the laws or customs of war, which include, but are not limited to, murder, ill-treatment, or deportation to slave-labour or for any other purpose of civilian population of or in occupied territory, murder or ill-treatment of prisoners of war or persons on the seas, killing of hostages, plunder of public or private property, wanton destruction of cities, towns, or villages, or devastation not justified by military necessity.

(c) *Crimes against humanity:*

Murder, extermination, enslavement, deportation and other inhuman acts done against any civilian population, or persecutions on political, racial, or religious grounds, when such acts are done or such persecutions are carried on in execution of or in connection with any crime against peace or any war crime.

Principle VII. Complicity in the commission of a crime against peace, a war crime, or a crime against humanity as set forth in Principle VI is a crime under international law.

Most citizens of Earth have set their sights too low in terms of recognizing global problems and seeking solutions. We need to lift our vision and see the Earth, as space explorers have, as a unique and wonderful life-supporting island in the vastness of space, worthy of being preserved.

We are all citizens of Earth because that is our birthright, but we are citizens without a government. The United Nations, as important and valuable as it is, represents only nations. The U.N. is a confederation of nations, and nations rather than individuals are its members. Most nations still operate under the illusion or delusion of sovereignty. But sovereignty is now shifting to where it has always truly belonged— to the Earth as a whole. Global cooperation has become the prerequisite to survival in the Nuclear Age.

RIGHTS AND RESPONSIBILITIES

As Earth citizens, we have both rights and responsibilities. Our rights exist under international law and include the Universal Declaration of Human Rights, which was adopted by the United Nations more than forty years ago on December 10, 1948. These rights, shown at the end of the chapter, were prepared in response to the gross violations of fundamental human rights during World War II. Article 3 of the Universal Declaration states, "Everyone has the right to life, liberty and the security of person." This right is clearly jeopardized by a continuing nuclear arms race with its hovering threat of omnicide.

Article 28 of the Universal Declaration provides that "Everyone is entitled to a social and international order in which the rights and freedoms set forth in this declaration can be fully realized." An international order in which some nations threaten nuclear holocaust in the name of their own "security" clearly has not met the required standards of this article. As Earth citizens, we must work to change offending national policies in order to claim the rights guaranteed to us in the Universal Declaration.

What are our responsibilities? Our most basic responsibility is to do our part to assure the survival of life on our planet and to be a positive link between the past and the future. To achieve this it will be necessary to do the following:

1. Adopt a global perspective.
2. Become educated about the dangers and threats to the Earth and its varied life forms.
3. Become an advocate of the Earth's well-being for all of its inhabitants.
4. Make a personal commitment to Earth stewardship, to preserving and protecting the planet for future generations.
5. Insist upon the global implementation of the Universal Declaration of Human Rights.
6. Insist upon a reallocation of national resources from destructive to constructive technologies and programs.
7. Hold national officials accountable under the Nuremberg Principles.
8. Support cooperative international programs aimed at reducing inequities among Earth citizens, regardless of nationality.
9. Speak out and educate others on issues of global survival and well-being.
10. Celebrate each day the wonder of life and the remarkable planet that supports it.

A "Declaration of Human Responsibilities for Peace and Sustainable Development" has been proposed by the Government of Costa Rica for universal adoption. This document deserves study, reflection, and public discussion.

We are all, for better or for worse, citizens of planet Earth. I contend that we must begin to take seriously our rights and responsibilities as citizens of Earth. We must begin to think and act as Earth citizens and teach our children to do so. We must also demand that each nation do so. Imagine a world in which children began each school day with the following variation of the U. S. pledge of allegiance: "I pledge allegiance to the Earth, and to its varied life forms; one world, indivisible, with liberty, justice and dignity for all."[6] It would be a start in creating the "new way of thinking" that Einstein warned us was necessary to avoid "unparalleled catastrophe."

For adults, I encourage adopting the following pledge as a guideline for living responsibly as Earth Citizens.

EARTH CITIZEN PLEDGE

Aware of the vastness of the universe and the uniqueness of life, I accept and affirm my responsibility as an Earth Citizen to nurture and care for our planet as a peaceful, harmonious home where life may flourish.

Believing that each of us can make a difference, I pledge to persevere in Waging Peace. With my spirit, intellect, and energy I shall strive to:

- *Reverse the nuclear arms race, and end this omnicidal threat to the continuation of life;*
- *Redirect scientific and economic resources from the destructive pursuit of weapons technologies to the beneficial tasks of ending hunger, disease, and poverty;*
- *Break down barriers between people and nations, and by acts of friendship, reduce tensions and suspicions;*
- *Live gently on the Earth, reclaiming and preserving the natural beauty and profound elegance of our land, mountains, oceans, and sky; and*
- *Teach others, by my words and deeds, to accept all members of the human family, and to love the Earth and live with dignity and justice upon it.*

INDIVIDUAL COMMITMENT

Earth citizenship exists in the realm of individual loyalty and commitment. There is no government of Earth to authorize or legitimatize Earth citizenship. Such legitimation of embracing Earth citizenship must come from within the individual and can arise only as a matter of conviction that such commitment is necessary to preserve the Earth and assure the survival of humanity in the Nuclear Age.

The world is in a process of transformation made necessary by the development and implementation of technologies too powerful to be controlled by any nation. Nuclear, chemical, biological, and communication technologies have rendered borders obsolete and thus nations incapable of solving serious global problems. These dying giants are struggling, however, to maintain their status, power, and political legitimacy in a world in which the impact of technology cannot be territorially confined. Thus, national leaders attempt to project the illusion of control within their territories while technological threats to the Earth and its inhabitants continue to become more pressing. Nuclear weapons threaten immediate catastrophe, and ecological mismanagement (or lack of management) threatens the slower and more painful destruction of the Earth and dislocation of its inhabitants. National borders and governmental machinery provide diminishing protection against foreseeable technologically induced disasters. Even the most powerful nations are helpless to effectively combat the destruction of the ozone layer, the alteration of the Earth's climate, or the initiation of nuclear war.

This analysis of increasing national impotence to deal with global threats suggests a paradox. If powerful nations are helpless before these threats, then must not relatively weak individuals be even more helpless? The answer is no. Individuals of all nations have become potential victims of decentralized territorially defined power in the global system. But individuals have greater potential than state actors (that is, other individuals who occupy and are constrained in their vision by roles of national leadership) to identify the threats to themselves inherent in the present system and take actions to reorient the global system to be responsive to these threats.

A recognition of the incapacity of nations to protect and preserve the Earth, and thus assure the survival of humanity, is inherent in an individual commitment to Earth citizenship. By giving allegiance to a global order, even before there exists the political and social structure to support it, the individual becomes a personal force for global change. When enough individuals have redefined their loyalties from the part to the whole, from the past to the future, the imperative for global problem-solving and management of technological threats will become unassailable. Toward that end, each of us who adopts the perspective of Earth citizenship and speaks and acts from this perspective will play a pioneering role in creating a world of peace, justice, and ecological well-being that is waiting to be born.

Enormous creativity and effort will be required to change the course of history toward a sane, safe, and sustainable future. It has always been my conviction that such a future is possible and achievable within the span of our lives. As threatening as the nuclear era is, it has provided us with the opportunity to work together to preserve our most important common heritage, the Earth.

UNIVERSAL DECLARATION OF HUMAN RIGHTS

Proclaimed by General Assembly Resolution 217 (III) of December 10, 1948.

Preamble

Whereas recognition of the inherent dignity and of the equal and inalienable rights of all members of the human family is the foundation of freedom, justice and peace in the world,

Whereas disregard and contempt for human rights have resulted in barbarous acts which have outraged the conscience of mankind, and the advent of a world in which human beings shall enjoy freedom of speech and belief and freedom from fear and want has been proclaimed as the highest aspiration of the common people,

Whereas it is essential, if man is not to be compelled to have recourse, as a last resort, to rebellion against tyranny and oppression, that human rights should be protected by the rule of law,

Whereas it is essential to promote the development of friendly relations between nations,

Whereas the peoples of the United Nations have in the Charter reaffirmed their faith in fundamental human rights, in the dignity and worth of the human person and in the equal rights of men and women and have determined to promote social progress and better standards of life in larger freedom,

Whereas Member States have pledged themselves to achieve, in cooperation with the United Nations, the promotion of universal respect for and observance of human rights and fundamental freedoms,

Whereas a common understanding of these rights and freedoms is of the greatest importance for the full realization of this pledge,

Now, therefore, The General Assembly
Proclaims this Universal Declaration of Human Rights as a common standard of achievement for all peoples and all nations, to the end that every individual and every organ of society, keeping this Declaration constantly in mind, shall strive by teaching and education to promote respect for these rights and freedoms and by progressive measures, national and international, to secure their universal and effective recognition and observance, both among the peoples of Member States themselves and among the peoples of territories under their jurisdiction.

ARTICLE 1
All human beings are born free and equal in dignity and rights. They are endowed with reason and conscience and should act towards one another in a spirit of brotherhood.

ARTICLE 2
Everyone is entitled to all the rights and freedoms set forth in this Declaration, without distinction of any kind, such as race,

colour, sex, language, religion, political or other opinion, national or social origin, property, birth or other status. Furthermore, no distinction shall be made on the basis of the political, jurisdictional or international status of the country or territory to which a person belongs, whether it be independent, trust, non-self-governing or under any other limitation of sovereignty.

ARTICLE 3
Everyone has the right to life, liberty and the security of person.

ARTICLE 4
No one shall be held in slavery or servitude; slavery and the slave trade shall be prohibited in all their forms.

ARTICLE 5
No one shall be subjected to torture or to cruel, inhuman or degrading treatment or punishment.

ARTICLE 6
Everyone has the right to recognition everywhere as a person before the law.

ARTICLE 7
All are equal before the law and are entitled without any discrimination to equal protection of the law. All are entitled to equal protection against any discrimination in violation of this Declaration and against any incitement to such discrimination.

ARTICLE 8
Everyone has the right to an effective remedy by the competent national tribunals for acts violating the fundamental rights granted him by the constitution or by law.

ARTICLE 9
No one shall be subjected to arbitrary arrest, detention or exile.

ARTICLE 10
Everyone is entitled in full equality to a fair and public hearing by an independent and impartial tribunal, in the determination of his rights and obligations and of any criminal charge against him.

ARTICLE 11
1. Everyone charged with a penal offence has the right to be presumed innocent until proved guilty according to law in a public trial at which he has had all guarantees necessary for his defence.
2. No one shall be held guilty of any penal offence on account of any act or omission which did not constitute a penal offence, under national or international law, at the time when it was committed. Nor shall a heavier penalty be imposed than the one that was applicable at the time the penal offence was committed.

ARTICLE 12
No one shall be subjected to arbitrary interference with his privacy, family, home or correspondence, nor to attacks upon his honour and reputation. Everyone has the right to the protection of the law against such interference or attacks.

ARTICLE 13
1. Everyone has the right to freedom of movement and residence within the borders of each State.
2. Everyone has the right to leave any country, including his own, and to return to his country.

ARTICLE 14
1. Everyone has the right to seek and to enjoy in other countries asylum from persecution.

2. This right may not be invoked in the case of prosecutions genuinely arising from nonpolitical crimes or from acts contrary to the purposes and principles of the United Nations.

ARTICLE 15
1. Everyone has the right to a nationality.
2. No one shall be arbitrarily deprived of his nationality nor denied the right to change his nationality.

ARTICLE 16
1. Men and women of full age, without any limitation due to race, nationality or religion, have the right to marry and to found a family. They are entitled to equal rights as to marriage, during marriage and at its dissolution.
2. Marriage shall be entered into only with the free and full consent of the intending spouses.
3. The family is the natural and fundamental group unit of society and is entitled to protection by society and the State.

ARTICLE 17
1. Everyone has the right to own property alone as well as in association with others.
2. No one shall be arbitrarily deprived of his property.

ARTICLE 18
Everyone has the right to freedom of thought, conscience and religion; this right includes freedom to change his religion or belief, and freedom, either alone or in community with others and in public or private, to manifest his religion or belief in teaching, practice, worship and observance.

ARTICLE 19
Everyone has the right to freedom of opinion and expression; this right includes freedom to hold opinions without interference

and to seek, receive and impart information and ideas through any media and regardless of frontiers.

ARTICLE 20

1. Everyone has the right to freedom of peaceful assembly and association.
2. No one may be compelled to belong to an association.

ARTICLE 21

1. Everyone has the right to take part in the government of his country, directly or through freely chosen representatives.
2. Everyone has the right of equal access to public service in his country.
3. The will of the people shall be the basis of the authority of government; this will shall be expressed in periodic and genuine elections which shall be by universal and equal suffrage and shall be held by secret vote or by equivalent free voting procedures.

ARTICLE 22

Everyone, as a member of society, has the right to social security and is entitled to realization, through national effort and international cooperation and in accordance with the organization and resources of each State, of the economic, social and cultural rights indispensable for his dignity and the free development of his personality.

ARTICLE 23

1. Everyone has the right to work, to free choice of employment, to just and favourable conditions of work and to protection against unemployment.
2. Everyone, without any discrimination, has the right to equal pay for equal work.

3. Everyone who works has the right to just and favourable remuneration ensuring for himself and his family an existence worthy of human dignity, and supplemented, if necessary, by other means of social protection.
4. Everyone has the right to form and to join trade unions for the protection of his interests.

ARTICLE 24
Everyone has the right to rest and leisure, including reasonable limitation of working hours and periodic holidays with pay.

ARTICLE 25
1. Everyone has the right to a standard of living adequate for the health and well-being of himself and of his family, including food, clothing, housing and medical care and necessary social services, and the right to security in the event of unemployment, sickness, disability, widowhood, old age or other lack of livelihood in circumstances beyond his control.
2. Motherhood and childhood are entitled to special care and assistance. All children, whether born in or out of wedlock, shall enjoy the same social protection.

ARTICLE 26
1. Everyone has the right to education. Education shall be free, at least in the elementary and fundamental stages. Elementary education shall be compulsory. Technical and professional education shall be made generally available and higher education shall be equally accessible to all on the basis of merit.
2. Education shall be directed to the full development of the human personality and to the strengthening of respect for human rights and fundamental freedoms. It shall promote understanding, tolerance and friendship among all nations, racial

or religious groups, and shall further the activities of the United Nations for the maintenance of peace.

3. Parents have a prior right to choose the kind of education that shall be given to their children.

ARTICLE 27

1. Everyone has the right freely to participate in the cultural life of the community, to enjoy the arts and to share in scientific advancement and its benefits.

2. Everyone has the right to the protection of the moral and material interests resulting from any scientific, literary or artistic production of which he is the author.

ARTICLE 28

Everyone is entitled to a social and international order in which the rights and freedoms set forth in this declaration can be fully realized.

ARTICLE 29

1. Everyone has duties to the community in which alone the free and full development of his personality is possible.

2. In the exercise of his rights and freedoms, everyone shall be subject only to such limitations as are determined by law solely for the purpose of securing due recognition and respect for the rights and freedoms of others and of meeting the just requirements of morality, public order and general welfare in a democratic society.

3. These rights and freedoms may in no case be exercised contrary to the purposes and principles of the United Nations.

ARTICLE 30

Nothing in this declaration may be interpreted as implying for any State, group or person any right to engage in any activity or to perform any act aimed at the destruction of any of the rights and freedoms set forth herein.

16 | FRANK K. KELLY
What Humanity Can Do: The Power of Citizens

Each year we observe the anniversary of a tragic event that shocked the world—the sudden destruction of a Japanese city, Hiroshima, by an atomic bomb made by citizens of the United States. The event produced repercussions all over this planet—and its repercussions will continue throughout the history of humanity.

Who must bear the responsibilities for the making of that bomb and dropping it upon the people of that city? Did its use and the explosion of another bomb on Nagasaki simply speed up the ending of World War II—or were those weapons designed to show the world that one nation, the USA, must dominate the Earth and control the future of the human race?

The historical evidence indicates that the bombs were built out of fear—fear that Adolf Hitler's Nazi scientists were developing such weapons. Albert Einstein, probably the greatest scientist of this century, sent a letter to President Roosevelt urging him to launch an atomic bomb project to beat the Nazis. When Harry Truman became president after Roosevelt's death, his advisors recommended that the bomb be used against a Japanese target as soon as possible. In his *Memoirs*, Truman showed his awe of it: "It was the achievement of the combined efforts of science, industry, labor, and the military, and it had no parallel in history. I never had any doubt that it should be used."

Billions of dollars had been poured into the development of that monstrous weapon. More than 100,000 persons had contributed their talents, their skills, their dedication to the project. Would it have been possible for an American president to have exploded such an astounding weapon over a desert island? Harry Truman was convinced by his advisors that a technical demonstration would not have brought Japan to its knees. Human lives had to be sacrificed.

How was it possible for Harry Truman, a good citizen, a dedicated servant of the American people, a man with high ideals and a deep belief in the value of life, to make such an horrendous decision? On a beautiful afternoon at the White House, in the spring of 1949, Mr. Truman explained his decision to me in these terms: "War is hell. Old General Sherman told us that in the Civil War. War is hell. We were at war with the Japanese. . . . We had given them a chance to surrender, and they had refused it. We were killing thousands of Japanese men, women, and children night after night with fire-bombs dropped from B-29's. I hated that, but we had to do it. We were preparing to invade Japan—to kill tens of thousands of Japanese soldiers and civilians, and to lose tens of thousands of our own men in that invasion. So I asked: How many people will this bomb kill if we drop it on a city? I was told we might kill 50,000 or 80,000 people, but it could end the war. It could give the emperor a chance to stop the fighting. So I made my decision, because I believed it would save many thousands of lives."

In World War II, the Japanese were often depicted as subhuman—as slant-eyed monsters, capable of tortures and cruelties that human beings would never sanction. And yet Allied bombers burned up thousands of men, women, and children in German and Japanese cities. We revealed in that war the limitless ability of human beings to inflict injuries and death upon those regarded as enemies.

Mr. Truman found it hard to understand why many commentators referred to the thousands of people killed or injured by atomic bombs, but did not mention the fact that millions of people were killed or wounded by so-called "conventional" weapons. Altogether, the estimates of deaths inflicted by these weapons range from 35 million to 60 million.

"I hope the world will not soon forget the terrible slaughter of human beings that went on in the six years of the Second World War," Mr. Truman said in his book, *Mr. Citizen.* "I hope we will remember the anguish and ravages visited upon civilian populations that were caused almost entirely by weapons that were regarded as 'conventional.' I abhor war and I am opposed to any kind of killing—whether by atomic bomb or bow and arrow. War is killing on a mass scale and it is war that we must eliminate—or it will eliminate us. . . . There is little hope for the future of the world unless we put an end to wars. . . . "

Truman hoped that the formation of the United Nations would lead to a world organization strong enough to prevent wars. When he campaigned for election in 1948, he said: "The fate of mankind depends on the foreign policy of the United States." He ran on a global platform that I helped to create. He declared: "The heart and soul of American foreign policy is peace. We are supporting a world organization to keep the peace, and a world economic policy to create prosperity for all nations."

In 1950, when the Korean War occurred, President Truman sent American troops to support the South Korean government and he obtained the endorsement of the United Nations for his policy. His hatred of war was genuine, and yet he felt that aggression had to be met by armed resistance if necessary. He insisted that "war—and the causes that lead to war—must be abolished."

He was deeply involved in the long struggle between the United States and the Soviet Union, but he was sure that the Soviet people and the American people could find a way to live together in peace. He firmly resisted the pressures brought upon him to engage in a military conflict with the Soviets. He said that what was at stake was "life or death, not only for ourselves and our children, but for our civilization."

"I think that in our lifetime we may hope to see a significant change take place in Russia," Truman said in 1960. "I have great faith in people, whatever their race or wherever they are."

I think that his faith in the people of the United States was a major factor in his amazing election victory in 1948. When I attended an early meeting of the campaign staff in Clark Clifford's office in the White House, Truman walked in and told us: "I'm going out to talk with the people. Don't be discouraged by the polls. The people will see that I'm a better man than Tom Dewey."

When Truman left the White House in January of 1953, he took delight in being called "Mr. Citizen." He declared that free citizens held the highest public offices in a true democracy. "When I was President, I was the people's hired hand," he told me. He was very proud of the Marshall Plan and the other cooperative programs carried out by his administration after World War II. Arnold Toynbee, the great British historian, once said that Truman's efforts to help many countries prosper in peace after that war should be called the most significant achievement of this century.

I mention these things because it is important to understand that Harry Truman was much more than the man who ordered the bombing of Hiroshima. He saw clearly that we Americans are linked with people everywhere on Earth—and we cannot solve humanity's problems without considering those people and working with them to solve the tremendous problems we now face.

My experience in the Truman campaign of 1948 strengthened my respect for the intelligence and compassion of my fellow citizens. I had never participated in a political campaign before that one. I had been a journalist, a reporter and editor for the *Kansas City Star* and the Associated Press. I had looked at politics as a "dirty business." Truman fought hard, but he did not engage in mudslinging. "I want to campaign on the facts," he said. "I want to get as many facts as I can into my speeches." He went across the country by train, visiting towns that had never seen a presidential candidate. Sometimes he spoke to hundreds of people who had gathered by the railroad tracks. Sometimes he spoke to small groups early in the morning. He treated them all with respect. He listened to their questions and he responded to them.

He was an admirer of President Woodrow Wilson, and I think he got from Wilson his realization that the American people had to be committed to human rights and the future of humanity. He carried in his wallet a poem by the English writer, Alfred Tennyson, entitled "Locksley Hall," composed in 1842. Tennyson wrote:

"For I dipt into the future, far as human eye could see,
Saw the Vision of the World, and all the wonder that could
  be;

Saw the heavens fill with commerce, argosies of magic
sails, Pilots of the purple twilight, dropping down with
costly bales;
Heard the heavens fill with shouting, and there rained a
ghastly dew
From the nations' airy navies grappling in the central
blue . . .
Till the war-drums throbb'd no longer, and the battle flags
were furled
In the Parliament of Man, the Federation of the
World . . . "

Many people in this country and in other nations supported the
War in the Persian Gulf because it was apparently fought under the
sponsorship of the United Nations. They believed that it showed
that the U.N. was at last becoming an effective "Federation of the
World." I think that many people now realize that they were deceived,
because the war inflicted terrible devastation on the people and the
environment in the Gulf area—and the U.N. is struggling to cope with
the awful consequences of the savage bombings conducted by the Allied forces.

Dr. Daniel Goleman—in a challenging book, *Vital Lies, Simple
Truths*—has reminded us that in many instances we seem to prefer
what he calls "vital lies" to the "simple truths" that may be too painful
for us to accept. He declares: "To let ourselves be guided by a sensi-
bility riven with blind spots, one twisted by the anxious need to avoid
truths, is to increase the rate of our acceleration toward disaster.
Truths must be told if we are to find our way out. Indeed, the clear and
strong voices of the lucid among us may be our last and best
hope. . . . "

I found "clear and strong voices" among the people who participated with me in the National Peace Academy Campaign, which led to
the creation of a United States Institute of Peace. With the active efforts of 45,000 citizens, we persuaded the Congress to establish that
institute over the opposition of President Reagan and David Stockman. That wonderful experience persuaded me that "we the people"

have the power to accomplish many changes in national and international affairs if we exercise the fundamental rights we have under our Constitution.

In a Foreword to the book we published on that campaign—called *The 100% Challenge*—Senator Mark Hatfield said:

> We acted on the understanding that peace is more than the absence of war: it is justice, and it is an ongoing process. In biblical terms, it is *shalom*—'Wholeness.' Never out of our thoughts were the children, those growing up under the shadow of nuclear annihilation and those we hope will come into and create a better world than ours. We also understood that every forty-five minutes, the world spends enough money just arming itself to operate the U.S. Institute of Peace for two years.
>
> The view that peace is secured by preparing for war could too easily consume any federal peace institution that was not insulated from the bureaucratic momentum of the central government. George Orwell, in *1984*, warned against corruption of language, when peace would simply be a different name for war. So we guarded against diversions, especially from political forces: the U.S. Institute of Peace will not participate in policy-making, and it will not intervene in disputes. Through research, education and training, and an information service, the Institute will focus on the elements and practical methods of peace among nations.
>
> We also wanted the Institute to belong to all Americans, whether or not questions of international peace are a direct part of their daily responsibilities, and we designed it carefully. We directed it to consider both government experience and that of the American people, particularly as we resolve local, regional, and national problems fairly and without violence. . . .
>
> The Institute's public mandate is based on democratic principles of citizen participation. We guide education, local welfare and safety, and state and national policy de-

cisions through parent-teacher associations, school boards, city councils, and the activities of state legislators and U.S. Representatives and Senators. In international affairs, however, our democratic ways are much less practiced. . . . Once we move past our borders into the more distant spheres of international relations and diplomacy, we seem to enter the territory of the specialist where there are signs that say 'off limits'. . . .

But leaving life-and-death decisions up to experts is risky and not to be tolerated in democracies. . . . Peace is more certain when the public achieves a voice in the nation's international activities. . . .

I am confident that, from the vantage-point of the twenty-first century, the seemingly small step we took to establish the U.S. Institute of Peace will be seen as one of the most important post-World War II acts of the U.S. government to bring peace to the world. . . .

In fact, it was an action taken by a reluctant government under the prodding of 45,000 citizens. The idea for a Peace Office had been around for nearly two hundred years. In the 1790s Dr. Benjamin Rush, a signer of the Declaration of Independence, and Benjamin Banneker, a black publisher and a noted mathematician, had tried to persuade Congress to establish a Peace Office on the same level as the War Department. They wanted to form "an office for promoting and preserving perpetual peace in our country. . . ."

As our bloody history shows, perpetual peace was not preserved in our country or elsewhere. We went through a grim Civil War, which changed the Constitution and abolished slavery, but left deep wounds still felt today. Under President Wilson's leadership, we participated in World War I "to end War" and "to make the world safe for democracy." As we all know, we have been involved in many military conflicts in recent years, including the recent slaughter in the Persian Gulf.

Yet the idea of preserving and promoting peace has remained alive in America. In the Bicentennial Year of 1976, Senators Hatfield and Harke introduced a bill to establish a George Washington Peace

Academy. An effort to support that action developed among private
citizens. Two physicians—Dr. Bryant Wedge and Dr. Jerome
Frank—and a Baltimore businessman, Nachman Gerber, formed the
Ad Hoc Committee for a National Peace Academy. That committee
launched the National Peace Academy Campaign.

Dr. Wedge invited me to become a director of that campaign and to
serve as co-chairman with him. I declined the chairmanship but I
served on the board of directors. Henry Burnett, a direct mail specialist, and I developed materials about the Peace Academy idea and obtained the funds to send letters to more than two million citizens. The
Campaign developed an active membership of 45,000 people, located
in all parts of the United States.

While the Peace Academy Campaign was under way, I was asked
to go to Moscow with twenty-one other citizens drawn from various religious groups to engage in a dialogue with Soviet leaders on ways to
end the nuclear arms race. I went as a representative of the Nuclear
Age Peace Foundation, which I helped to establish in Santa Barbara
in 1982 with Dr. David Krieger, a political scientist; Wallace Drew,
an investment broker; Kent Ferguson, a school administrator; and
Charles Jamison, an attorney. The arms race was then at its height,
with enormous numbers of new weapons being built and hostility rising between the U.S. and the Soviet Union.

In Moscow on April 26, 1983, in an address to seventy-nine Soviet
officials, I urged them to take the lead in a great movement for peace
by dismantling 50 percent of their nuclear weapons and inviting representatives of all the nations to come and witness that dismantling. I
urged them to open up their society, to take bold steps to end the so-
called "Cold War." I was deeply encouraged by their responses. I had
no idea then that Mikhail Gorbachev would emerge as a Soviet president with the courage and vision to go far beyond what I had suggested.

I spoke in Moscow as a free citizen, believing that Harry Truman
was right when he said that a citizen holds the highest office in the
United States. As a man who served in the American army in World
War II, I witnessed the carnage and the devastation caused by the
frightful weapons we used in that war. I shared Truman's view that a

war between the United States and the Soviet Union, with both sides capable of using nuclear weapons, would mean the end of civilization.

In that Moscow meeting I had to admit that I had participated in the shaping of the arms race. After I worked for Truman, I became the assistant to the Majority Leader of the U.S. Senate and staff director of the Majority Policy Committee. Year after year, the Senate approved enormous expenditures for arms. I talked with senators who realized that another world war would be an utter disaster for humanity—but they voted for the arms, because they believed that the Soviets were planning to dominate the world. I went along with that thinking for a long time. I deceived myself, and I did not challenge the self-deceptions of the senators.

When I realized that both political parties in the Senate were unable to come to grips with the real problems of humanity, I resigned with a feeling of disgust. In subsequent years I took on various projects—serving as the Washington director of Averell Harriman's presidential campaign in 1952; helping the American Book Publishers Council beat off censorship movements in 1954; and working as the U.S. Director of the International Press Institute's Study of World News.

I became involved in the peace movement on an international scale when I persuaded Robert Hutchins, president of the Center for the Study of Democratic Institutions, to convene an international convocation based on Pope John XXIII's encyclical, *Pacem in Terris* (Peace on Earth). Pope John tossed nuclear arms, nationalism, colonialism, racism, and nonconstitutional regimes into history's wastebasket. He threw aside the devil theory in politics. He declared that "the same moral law which governs relations between individual human beings serves also to regulate the relations of political communities with each other."

Dr. Hutchins, a Protestant educator who came from a long line of Presbyterians, explained why he agreed to sponsor a conference based on a papal statement. He said: "The reason why the encyclical is refreshing is that it breaks through the cliche curtain and talks a kind of hard, common sense. It refers to 'practical measures' and the 'management of affairs.'"

Hutchins continued: "The Pope is equally unfashionable in refusing to see power as the object of politics. *The object is the common good, that good which accrues to every person because he (or she) is a member of the community....* And finally the Pope maintains that no nation is any longer capable of serving the common good. We are all members of one community, we share one common destiny, the common good we seek is the good of the human community. We must now supply the political fabric of an existing world community, and the place to begin, as the Pope says, is the United Nations."

The convocation brought together two thousand participants from the United States and many other countries. Our speakers included U Thant, the Secretary-General of the U.N.; the president of the U.N. General Assembly and two former presidents; the Vice President of the U.S. and the Chief Justice of the Supreme Court; four U.S. Senators, including Claiborne Pell, now chairman of the Senate Foreign Relations Committee; leading officials from Russia, Yugoslavia, Poland, Belgium, Italy, and Israel; two justices of the World Court; Arnold Toynbee, a historian; and Paul Tillich, one of the world's great Protestant theologians.

In an article in *Life* magazine, John K. Jessup described the convocation in these words: "An extraordinary assemblage of the world's movers and shakers converged on New York City to grapple with a staggeringly ambitious subject: solutions to the eternal human problem of war."

In my view, the most moving statement was made by Abba Eban, then the deputy prime minister of Israel. Eban said: "War has too often been regarded as a part of man's essential nature, the source of nobility, heroism, and redeeming sacrifice.... Today the ideal of peace converges with its necessity.... Everything in history that once made for war now makes for peace. In this I include our new and all-pervading vulnerability." Eban called for an annual assembly of governmental leaders "to survey not the state of any nation but the state of mankind."

"As we look out on the human condition, our consciences cannot be clean," Eban said. "If they are clean, then it is because we do not use them enough. It is not inevitable that we march in hostile and separated hosts into the common abyss. There is another possibility—of an ordered world, illumined by reason and governed by law. If we cannot yet touch it with our hands let us, at least, grasp it in our vision."

In 1967 I wrote an article for *The Center Magazine* advocating an annual report on the state of mankind to be presented on global television by the Secretary-General of the U.N. At the invitation of Norman Cousins, I summarized this proposal in an editorial in *The Saturday Review*. It was endorsed by former President Dwight Eisenhower, fifteen U.S. senators, and leaders in many fields; but bureaucrats in the U.N. organization regarded it as "dangerous" and "controversial" and prevented U Thant from launching it. Cousins informed me that U Thant was ready to do it, but the implementation of the report was blocked by his associates.

In 1988, at the suggestion of a supporting member of the Nuclear Age Peace Foundation, I asked for a reconsideration of the idea. In a proposal published by that foundation, I wrote:

> If our air is being polluted, our climate is being changed, our resources are being wasted on guns and bombs, if our Earth is being ravaged, as scientists know that it is— should not the voices of humanity be heard?
>
> The Secretary-General could convene a Summit Meeting for Humanity in Geneva or in the General Assembly Hall in New York. He could open the meeting by reviewing the planetary problems that require global cooperation —and give his personal statement on what might be done. He could speak with all the knowledge available to him from many nations, but he could also speak forthrightly as a person, as a human being with family and friends, standing before the people of the world as a Citizen of Humanity, calling upon all human beings to join in saving the Earth.
>
> Representatives of international organizations could then present reports from the fields of health, food and agriculture, disarmament and development, the arts, human rights, the global environment, and other areas of human activity. The needs of the Earth could be presented com-

prehensively by men and women with deep resources of information and wisdom. The sessions of the Summit for Humanity could be broadcast around the world in many languages. . . . "

In 1989, I had an opportunity to discuss the idea again at an international conference sponsored by the U.N.'s University for Peace in San Jose, Costa Rica. I spoke to six hundred participants from thirty nations. I said: "This Earth is ours. We live in a web of life that extends from continent to continent. We breathe air that moves across oceans and leaps mountains. *We live in one world—and we must act upon that fact.*"

I like to think that I helped to pave the way for the Earth Summit meeting sponsored by the U.N. in Brazil in June of 1992. I videotaped a statement in Santa Barbara, for possible use at that conference— declaring that all nuclear weapons should be placed under the authority of the United Nations—and calling on the U.N. to supervise and monitor the dismantling of the nuclear time bombs that are among the greatest threats to the world's environment.

As you can tell from this recital of my concern and projects, I enjoy speaking out as a free citizen. My latest effort is to create a National Council of Citizens to put new life into our half-paralyzed democracy.

It is evident that our elected leaders will not consider drastic decisions until large numbers of citizens call for new policies. Their experience has made them wary of us. They are not convinced that many of us are willing to take part in the grueling efforts that will be required to deal with the national and global problems we have neglected.

Is it true—as many commentators claim—that we are a greedy, corrupt, lazy, arrogant, ignorant people, unwilling to make sacrifices, unwilling to give our time and thought (and some of our resources) to what needs to be done? Have most of us really decided to "take the money and run"? Are we willing to go on permitting "spin doctors" and "media wizards" to make our elections meaningless farces, with the victors winning by tricks and deceptions?

Millions of people participated in the celebrations of Earth Day last spring. How many of us are ready to make a strong effort to restore "government of the people, by the people, for the people"—before we slide into economic and social chaos?

A nonpartisan National Council of Citizens—with chapters in every community—could shake up the two old parties, engage in a search for new leaders with new visions, and work creatively with people of other nations to get rid of nuclear weapons, to save our environment, and to move toward the abolition of poverty, oppression, and humanity's most terrible scourge—*War.*

This Council of Citizens could draw upon the information, ideas, and energies now being generated by many civic organizations— Common Cause, the Sierra Club and other environmental organizations, the League of Women Voters, the Public Citizen groups, the Mothers for Peace, and others—to generate a nonpartisan national program for "Action for Humanity in the Nuclear Age."

It should have two primary goals—to make the Office of Citizen recognized as the highest office in a true democracy, and to counteract the arrogance of elected and nonelected officials and "experts" who assert that the people have lost the will and the wisdom to make the hard choices that must be made.

It should convene Citizens' Assemblies at the end of each year—in all regions of the country, linked by satellite communications—to examine the records of Congress and the president in dealing with the needs of the people. The president and leaders of Congress would be asked to present reports to these assemblies and to answer questions from citizens. The assemblies could then criticize or commend the records of our public servants and also make recommendations for better policies.

Such a Council of Citizens could bring at least a million—and perhaps ten million—alienated Americans back into active efforts to make ours a fully self-governing democracy. It could restore the dignity of Cctizenship and offer the people of the world new hope for the future of America and the future of hundreds of millions of people who cling to the promises of democracy around the Earth.

The development of creative citizenship is one of the educational programs encouraged by the Nuclear Age Peace Foundation. The foundation itself came into existence as a result of a series of dialogues by citizens in Santa Barbara.

The foundation has produced a Magna Carta for the Nuclear Age— a charter of rights and responsibilities. The charter calls for the establishment of an International Criminal Court as a step toward the prevention of war and other crimes against humanity. Under its provisions all individuals, including heads of state and other high governmental officials, are to be held accountable for criminal violations of international law.

It is my hope that a Council of Citizens will foster support for the Magna Carta and other projects for the benefit of the World Community now emerging on this planet.

I hope that the council will seek a verifiable ban on all nuclear weapons testing. A comprehensive ban on all such tests would be the biggest single step toward reversing the nuclear arms race.

Other projects worthy of consideration by the Citizens' Council are:

- Establishing Accidental Nuclear War Assessment Centers to develop ways to reduce the risks of accidental firing of nuclear weapons systems;
- Urging Congress and the president to support global reductions in armaments and troops, led by the U.S. and the former Soviet Union;
- Placing the transfer of all weapons and components of weapons under strict international controls;
- Developing a planetary program to redirect the trillion dollars currently spent annually on arms to provide for the long-neglected needs of humanity;
- Revitalizing the United Nations—improving U.N. activities for human security, environmental protection, economic development;
- Requesting an annual Report on the State of Humanity, presented by the U.N. Secretary-General in cooperation with many nongovernmental organizations;
- Insisting that the president, Congress, and all governmental agencies respect the rights of citizens to have necessary information on all issues affecting their lives.

In the past two years, we have learned that human beings are capable of breaking the shackles of tyranny, astounding the "experts." The people of Western Europe are building a Community, despite the skepticism of the pundits who said that it couldn't be done. In Eastern Europe, the people smashed old systems and are now developing new ones. In Latin America, tremendous changes are occurring. In South Africa, the walls of apartheid are falling down.

We live in difficult and dangerous times. In this century, there have been two world wars, many revolutions, and upheavals everywhere. But the spirit of freedom has never been completely crushed. The creative strength of humanity has burst forth in every generation. Terrible times show what human beings can do.

The philosopher-historian William Irwin Thompson has described the surge of creative change in these terms: "The creation of a just world order. . . is already coming about through the spiritual transformation of consciousness in the mind of humanity in resonance with the mind of God."

In our materialistic age it is difficult for us to deal with such phrases as "the mind of humanity" and "the mind of God." Thompson bases his definitions on the work of Gregory Bateson, the systems theorist. In his seminal book, *Steps to an Ecology of Mind*," Bateson wrote: "The individual mind is immanent but not only in the body. It is immanent also in pathways and messages outside the body; and there is a larger mind of which the individual mind is only a subsystem. This larger mind is comparable to God and is perhaps what some people mean by 'God'. . ."

Most of us who watch television or listen to radios know that the air around us is filled with invisible images and sound waves we cannot hear without receivers. But it is not easy for us to accept the idea that our individual minds are receiving and transmitting thoughts to all the other minds invisibly linked together in what Bateson called "the total interconnected social system and planetary ecology." For many people, it is even more difficult to believe that there is "a larger mind" working in us and around us and in the entire social system and the whole planet.

Because we usually consider ourselves as separate persons with private thoughts and private destinies, we may quickly reject Dr. Bateson's description of our situation in a vastly mysterious universe. Yet the findings of many scientists have revealed the hidden connections that exist within us and between us.

Albert Einstein, who changed the lives of all of us by unlocking the huge energy of the atom, once declared: "Everyone who is seriously involved in the pursuit of science becomes convinced that a spirit is manifest in the laws of the universe—a spirit vastly superior to that of man, and one in the face of which we, with our modest powers, must be humble."

Einstein was not a conventionally religious man, but he was awed by what he had learned about the amazing qualities of the universe. He did not think that scientists could ever penetrate its ultimate secrets. He realized that humanity was engaged in an endless voyage of discovery with limitless possibilities. With other notable scientists, he admitted that many leaps of the mind had occurred in flashes of insight that could not be explained.

What humanity can do is beyond anything we imagine in our present circumstances. We live in an age in which ideas are circulating around the world at unprecedented speed. No one can control them; no barriers can stop them. No one can anticipate what will come from the mind of humanity resonating with the Larger Mind that Einstein found to be operating in the universe on a tremendous scale.

Christopher Fry, in his play *A Sleep of Prisoners*, offers us reasons for confidence in these marvelous lines:

"Thank God our time is now
When wrong comes up to meet us everywhere
Never to leave us until we take
The greatest stride of soul . . ."

I see signs that we are taking what the poet called "the greatest stride of soul." These are times of great sufferings and great transformations.

Henri Bergson, the French philosopher, once said: "The art of governing a great people is the only one for which there exists no technical training, no effective education. . . ." In the coming age, the age of fulfillment for humanity, "we the people" will learn together that we must develop the "art of governing" by accepting our responsibilities and demonstrating what we can do as citizens working together for the good of all.

NOTES

INTRODUCTION

1. David Adams, "The Seville Statement on Violence: A Progress Report," *Journal of Peace Research* 26, no. 2 (1989): 113-121.

2. Center for Defense Information, "U.S. Military Agenda for 1992 and Beyond," *The Defense Monitor* 10, no. 6 (1991).

3. Diana Hull, "Informed Consent, From the Body to the Body-Politic in the Nuclear Age" in *Waging Peace in the Nuclear Age,* ed. David Krieger and Frank K. Kelly (Santa Barbara: Capra Press, 1988), 49-66.

CHAPTER 6

1. Javier Perez de Cuellar, Foreword to *The Gaia Peace Atlas, Survival into the Third Millennium,* ed. Dr. Frank Barnaby (New York: Doubleday, 1988), 8.

2. Frank Barnaby, ed., *The Gaia Peace Atlas, Survival into the Third Millennium* (New York: Doubleday, 1988), 14.

3. Ibid., 16.

4. Ibid., 26.

5. Ibid., 18.

CHAPTER 7

1. Harvey Wasserman and Norman Soloman, *Killing Our Own: the Disaster of America's Experience with Atomic Radiation* (New York: Delacorte Press, 1982).

2. Ibid.

3. "Christian Conscience and Modern War," an editorial from *Civilta Cattolica,* 6 July 1991, pp. 3-16.

4. William Johnston, *Letters to Conntemplatives* (London: Fount Paperbacks, HarperCollins Publishing Group, 1991).

5. C. McCarthy, "The Theology and Spirituality of Christian Non-Violence," Workshop materials available from Fr. Charlie McCarthy, 49 Burkeside Avenue, Brockton, Massachusetts 02401.

6. Thomas Merton, *Faith and Violence* (Notre Dame, IN: University of Notre Dame Press, 1968), 6-7.

7. George Wald, "The Arms Race: How to Stop It and What Stands In Its Way," speech available from: Promoting Enduring Peace, P.O. Box 5103, Woodmont, Connecticut 06460.

8. Bob Aldridge, "Trident Today," *Ground Zero* (Spring, 1992).

9. Theodore Hesburgh, Speech to Business Executives for National Security, 9 October 1991, at Stanford, Connecticut.
10. Martin Luther King, Jr., "Prayers for Ecumenical Celebration of Creation."
11. "Prayers for Ecumenical Celebration."

CHAPTER 9

1. If the motive had been to shorten the war by demonstrating the power of the new weapon, the bomb could have been exploded in an unpopulated area in sight of Tokyo, and this was Teller's recommendation. Secretary Stimson's diaries and other sources threw some light on the decision in later years. See P.M.S. Blackett: *Fear, War, and the Bomb: Military and Political Consequences of Atomic Energy* (New York: Whittlesey House, 1948); Len Giovanetti and Fred Freed: *The Decision to Drop the Bomb* (New York: Coward-McCann, 1965). For a fascinating analysis and guide to bibliography, see chapter 9 of H. Bruce Franklin: *War Stars: The Superweapon and the American Imagination* (New York: Oxford University Press, 1988).
2. Committee for Responsible Genetics, 186 South Street (4th Floor), Boston, Massachusetts 02111.
3. The Institute for Social Inventions, 24 Abercorn Place, London NW8 9XP.
4. For discussion of existing codes of professional ethics see: Stephen H. Unger, *Controlling Technology* (New York: Holt, Rinehart & Winston, New York, 1982); Mark S. Frankel, ed., *Values and Ethics in Organization and Human Systems Development* (Washington DC: AAAS, 1987).
5. See, for example, Karl Grossman and Judith Long, "Plutonium Con," *The Nation* 249 (1989): 589.
6. The issues raised by the involvement of academic research with the military are surveyed in several articles in *Science for the People* 20, no. 1 (1988).

CHAPTER 10

1. Carl Sagan "Great Peace March," *Waging Peace Series Booklet*, no. 11, Nuclear Age Peace Foundation (Santa Barbara: 1987).
2. See "Design and Action for a New World," available from the World Constitution and Parliament Association, 1480 Hoyt Street, Lakewood, Colorado 80215.
3. The case name is *In re: More than 50,000 Nuclear Weapons; The People of the Earth v. China, et al.* PDWC No. LA-83-0001; the case can be cited as *Los Angeles Daily Journal*, 29 August 1988, sec. 1, p. 1, wherein the case was discussed and briefly quoted. General articles also appeared in the *Los Angeles Times*, 24 November 1984, sec. 2, p. 8 (Valley News) and 24 July 1988, sec. I, p. 23.

4. The Boyle Opinion, as issued by the Court, 4-5.

5. *International Court of Justice; Acts and Documents Concerning the Organization of the Court*, no. 4, Charter of the United Nations, Statute and Rules of Court and Other Documents (1978), 77: Article 38(1) reads as follows: "1. The Court, whose function is to decide in accordance with international law such disputes as are submitted to it, shall apply:

(a) international conventions, whether general or particular, establishing rules expressly recognized by the contesting States;

(b) international custom, as evidence of a general practice accepted as law;

(c) the general principles of law recognized by civilized nations;

(d) subject to the provisions of Article 59, judicial decisions and the teachings of the most highly qualified publicists of the various nations, as subsidiary means for the determination of rules of law."

6. *Los Angeles Daily Journal*, 29 August 1988, sec. 1, p. 1, et seq.: "James Malone, Navy Chair of International Law at the Naval Postgraduate School in Monterey, said the provisional court decision could be recognized as a secondary source of international law." Ibid., p. 22. "Professor Edwin M. Smith of the USC Law Center said the provisional court hearing was 'a good thing to do. . . . There's absolutely no way to get the issues heard in any existing forum,' he said." Ibid.

7. The Boyle Opinion, as issued by the Court, 2.

8. Ibid., 5-6.

9. Ibid., 14.

10. Ibid., 22-23.

11. The Rubin Opinion, as issued by the Court, 12-13.

12. Ibid., 24-26.

13. The Weston Opinion, as issued by the Court, 3-4.

14. Ibid., 5.

15. Ibid., 7-8.

16. Ibid., 11.

CHAPTER 13

1. Jan Tinbergen, *World Security and Equity* (Brookfield, VT.: Edward Elgar Publishing Ltd, Gower Publishing Company, 1990).

2. Ibid.

3. R. Summers, et al., "Changes in the World Income" *Journal of Policy Modeling* 6 (1984): 237-270.

4. H. Thiel, "The Development of International Inequality, 1960-1985," *Journal of Econometrics* 42 (1989): 145-155.

5. H. W. Singer, "The Day of Reckoning Has Come," *Financial Times*, 18 October 1989.

6. Victor L. Urquidi, "A Proposal to Create a System for Part-Payment in Local Currency of Interest on External Debt," El Colegio de Mexico, Mexico D.F., Mexico.

7. Gro Harlem Bruntland, et al., *Our Common Future* (Oxford and New York: Oxford University Press, 1987).

8. United Nations, Official Records: Forty-third Session, Supplement no. 11 (A/43/11).

9. "U.S. Contributions to International Organizations, Report to the Congress for Fiscal Year 1984," Released December 1985 to President of the Senate, George Bush.

10. W. Brandt, et al., *North-South: A Programme for Survival* (London and Sydney: Pan Books, 1980).

11. Olof Palme, et al., *Common Security - A Blueprint for Survival* (New York: Simon and Schuster, 1982), 161-162.

12. *Our Common Future.*

13. G. Van Benthem van den Bergh, *The Taming of the Great Powers* (diss., University of Amsterdam, 1988).

14. J. Tinbergen, "Revitalizing the United Nations System," *Waging Peace Series Booklet*, no. 13, Nuclear Age Peace Foundation (Santa Barbara: 1987).

CHAPTER 14

1. R. J. Rummel, "Power Kills; Absolute Power Kills Absolutely," Haiku Institute of Peace Research (Honolulu: 1991).

2. The philosopher John Somerville coined the term "omnicide."

3. Francis Boyle, "The Criminality of Nuclear Weapons," *Waging Peace Series Booklet*, no. 27, Nuclear Age Peace Foundation (Santa Barbara, CA: 1991).

4. David Krieger, *Disarmament and Development, The Challenge of the International Control and Management of Dual-Purpose Technologies*, Foundation Reshaping the International Order (RIO) (Rotterdam, The Netherlands: 1981). Also see David Krieger, ed., *Disarmament and Development, Seven Dual-Purpose Technologies: An Assessment of Their Potential*, Foundation Reshaping the International Order (RIO) (Rotterdam, The Netherlands: 1981).

5. Jan Tinbergen, "Supranational Decision-Making: A More Effective United Nations," *Waging Peace Series Booklet*, no. 29, Nuclear Age Peace Foundation (Santa Barbara, CA: 1991).

6. "Declaration of Human Responsibilities for Peace and Sustainable Development," United Nations General Assembly Document A/44/626, 11 October 1989.

7. Cited in *Nazi Conspiracy and Aggression - Opinion and Judgment*

(Washington, D.C.: Government Printing Office, 1947), 172.

8. "Hearing Before the Committee on Foreign Relations, U. S. Senate, 102d Cong., 1st sess." (Washington, D.C.: Government Printing Office, 1991), 5-6.

9. "A Magna Carta for International Economic Development, Rights and Responsibilities," Foundation for the Establishment of an International Criminal Court (Santa Barbara: 1989).

CHAPTER 15

1. See Lester R. Brown, et. al., eds., *State of the World* (New York: W.W. Norton & Co). This report is issued annually.

2. See Helen Caldicott, *Missile Envy* (New York: Bantam Books, 1984).

3. State Department Report PPS/23 as quoted in Joseph Gerson, "The Quest for Disarmament in a Changing World," *Non-Violent Activist* (January/February 1989): 3.

4. See Lester R. Brown, et al., "No Time to Waste, A Global Agenda for the Bush Administration," *World-Watch* (January/February 1989): 10-19.

5. See Jan Tinbergen "Revitalizing the United Nations System" in *Waging Peace in the Nuclear Age, Ideas for Action,* eds. David Krieger and Frank Kelly (Santa Barbara, CA: Capra Press, 1988).

6. The Women's Foreign Policy Council has developed a Pledge of Allegiance to the Family of Earth: "I pledge allegiance to the Earth, and to the flora, fauna and human life that it supports, one planet, indivisible, with safe air, water and soil, economic justice, equal rights and peace for all."

NUCLEAR AGE PEACE
FOUNDATION CONTRIBUTORS

Margaret A. De Mott
Pallo and Lillian Deftereos
Rev. John C. DeMaagd
Richard Dennison
Bud Deraps
Loren and Jean DeVilbiss
Mr. and Mrs. Harry Diamond
H. George Dobriner
Diane B. Doiron
Richard J. Dovgin
Ellen Downing
Wallace T. Drew
Wallace T. Drew, Jr.
Audra A. Dusseau
Frances A. Dwight
Jane S. Dyruff
Diane and John Eckstein
Judy and Rob Egenolf
David and Patrice Ekstrom
Howard and Jay Elliott
Julia Emerson
M. M. Eskandari-Qajar
Genevieve Estes
Richard A. Falk
Kenneth Falstrom
Frances T. Farenthold
Sara J. Madjd Faridi
E. T. Feldsted
Ben Ferencz
Kent Ferguson
Leo D. Fialkoff
Sam and Louise Fields
David and Zelda Fields
Dietrich Fischer
R. E. Fisher
Mildred Flacks
Jeffrey G. Fleeman
Arthur and Anne Flor
Jason Floyd
J. Thomas Fly/Bank of Mont.
Cecile A. Forbes
David Forden

Rebecca G. Forsyth
Paul and Percilla Frank
Anthony M. Frank
Dr. and Mrs. David F. Frankel
Elaine Friedrich
Barbara J. Frombola
Morjorie P. Frost
H. Clark Fuller
Jeanne Gagnebin
Mr. and Mrs. L. H. Gamble
John H. Gaylord
Thomas R. Gentry
Margaret M. Getman
Mrs. V. C. Gillespie
Daniel Glaser
Samuel M. Glenn
Edward and Jeanne Green
Robert Y. Gromet, M.D.
Patrick Guilfoyle
Joseph Guilfoyle
Mary Rita Guilfoyle
Mabel A. Gunderson
Peggy Gustafson
Rev. and Mrs. Geo. J. Hall
Frances Halpern
Lois V. Hamer
Mark and Sally Hamilton
Mrs. C. E. Hanshew
Paul and Helen Hansma
Covington Hardee
Mr. Thomas J. Harriman
Robert C. Harrison
Clementina Cota Hart
Colin B. Hayward
Sven Hellman
Ursula E. Henderson, M.D.
Norman Hendry
Irene W. Henry
Ronalee Herrmann
Emma B. Heske
Harold J. Hicks
Richard Hirsch

Brett Hodges
Andora Hodgin
Gene Knudsen Hoffman
Julius and Sibyl Holder
Mrs. Dorothy Holland-Kaupp
Mrs. Jerome F. Houlis
John Iwerks
Charles W. Jamison
Len Jarrott
Marty Jenkins
Paul and Jean Johnson
William and Mabel Kalis
Fred and Megan Karlin
Dennis and Sylvia Karzag
Alan F. Kay
Nadia Kelada
Gene and Maryellen Kelley
Frank and Barbara Kelly
Mary and Terry Kelly
Stephen Kelly
Dr. and Mrs. Earl Kernahan
Audrey King
Katharine H. Kinkade
Ned and Ethel Kirkham
Bernard Kirtman
R. B. Klausner
Fred Knelman
Walter and Mara Kohn
Frances Komoroske
Stefan Krayk
David and Carolee Krieger
Herbert and Dorothy Krieger
Jane and Al Krieger
Daniel and Diane Krieger-Carlisle
Roger and Sue Kritz
Kroc Institute for International
    Peace Studies
Larry Laborde
Manfred Lachs
Dr. Stephan E. Lackner
Marshall Lamore
Ken and Lois Landau

David and Sharon Landecker
Mervin Lane
Frances D. Larkin
Eulah Laucks
Mr. and Mrs. Zola Lefcourt and
    Son
Howard S. Levy
The Rev. Dr. Richard C. Lief
Carolyn Coulter Liesy
Leatrice Lifshitz
Gary Lipton
Joseph and Sheila Lodge
C.R. and Mickey Loepkey
Mindy Lorenz
Eli Luria
Steve and Dana MacMillan
Mr. and Mrs. Robert W. Mairs
Patricia Masilo
Roger Mayer
Catherine McCann
Mr. and Mrs. Thomas McClure
James L. McFarling
E. Ann McGraw
Dr. and Mrs. John T. McGwire
Carol L. McLean
Mrs. Ernest Menzies
Rufus E. Miles, Jr.
Carole L. Milligan, M.D.
M. Joy Mills
Mr. and Mrs Clarence Minnerly
Barbara Morel
Lisa Moreno
Kenjiro Moriguchi
Mr. and Mrs. Ed Morin
Dorothy C. Morrell
Maryanne Mott and Herman Warsh
E. Schilling Mullin
Philip F. Murray, M.D.
Prudence R. Myer
Elly and Jack Nadel
Farzeen Nasri
Marjorie Navidi

Nebraskans for Peace
Mr. and Mrs. Ray Newbery
Hanna Newcombe
Aaron Nisenson
Lessie Sinclair Nixon
Genevieve Nowlin
The Nuclear Age Resource Center
Thomas and Lillian O'Reilly
Violet Oaklander
E. George and Vivian Obern
Imelda O'Brien
Mr. and Mrs. Robert S. Ogilvie
Mark Oliver
Arne Olsen
Eleanor and Sidney Ottman
Barbara Paarmann
Mr. and Mrs. Gerald B. Parent
Elizabeth Parker
Donald and Julieta Parsons, M.D.
J. R. Parten
Katy Peake
Mrs. Retta Peattie
Helen L. Pedotti
Julianne Pell
Ms. Dana Penoff
Paul Perlmutter
Mr. and Mrs. Robert Peterson
D. R. Phillips
Alan F. Phillips
Hank and Susan Pitcher
Kenneth J. Pitts
Jean C. Platt
Mr. and Mrs. Darryl Ponicsan
Mr. and Mrs. Warren E. Preece
Ilene Pritikin
Bill Raffin
Mr. and Mrs. Don Ralston
Bernard and Audre Rapoport
Gail Rappaport
Richard C. Raymond
Dr. Andrew A. Recsei
Doris Read

Elke Reimer
Walter and Esther Relis
Lyle G. Reynolds
Dennis Rice/Happy Valley School
Pauline M. Richards
Fred and Andrea Rifkin
Peter Robertson
James W. Robertson
Dr. and Mrs. Miles H. Robinson
Kerry Rodgers
Patricia Roelle
Gerda Rohden
Arden Rose
Kermit Rose
Mary Rose
Edward Rudin, M.D.
Peter Ruklie
SANA
Mr and Mrs Richard Sanford
Joan M. Saniuk
Maxine H. Sasso
Mr. and Mrs. Brooke Sawyer
Iva M. Schatz
Joseph Scher
Alan M. Schlenger
Margi and Larry Schneider
Dr. and Mrs. Arent H. Schuyler, Jr.
Glenn T. and Helen Seaborg
Mrs. Martin Serra
Sigrid Sharp
Ronald Shlensky, M.D.
Ms. S. Shoresman
Hallam C. Shorrock, Jr.
Mrs. George Sidenberg, Jr.
Janet Silverfarb
Herbert A. Simon
Bennet Skewes-Cox
Florence Smiler
Dr. Cedric A. B. Smith
Gregory S. Sommer
Stefen A. Sorsoli
Sybil Spencer